CBSE Term II
2022

Physical Education

Class XI

CBSE Term II 2022

Physical Education

Class XI

- Complete Theory is Sync with Syllabus
- Case Based Questions
- Short/Long Answer Type Questions
- 3 Practice Papers with Explanations

Authors
Reena Kar
Tushar Shukla

arihant

ARIHANT PRAKASHAN (School Division Series)

ARIHANT PRAKASHAN (School Division Series)

 **Administrative & Production Offices**

Regd. Office
'Ramchhaya' 4577/15, Agarwal Road, Darya Ganj, New Delhi -110002
Tele: 011- 47630600, 43518550

ॐ **Head Office**
Kalindi, TP Nagar, Meerut (UP) - 250002, Tel: 0121-7156203, 7156204

ॐ **Sales & Support Offices**
Agra, Ahmedabad, Bengaluru, Bareilly, Chennai, Delhi, Guwahati, Hyderabad, Jaipur, Jhansi, Kolkata, Lucknow, Nagpur & Pune.

ॐ **ISBN :** 978-93-25796-84-3

PO No : TXT-XX-XXXXXXX-X-XX

Published by Arihant Publications (India) Ltd.

For further information about the books published by Arihant, log on to www.arihantbooks.com or e-mail at info@arihantbooks.com

Follow us on    

Contents

Syllabus CBSE Term II Class XI

UNIT NO.	NAME

4. **PHYSICAL EDUCATION & SPORTS FOR CWSN**
(Children With Special Needs- Divyang)

- Aims & objectives of Adaptive Physical Education
- Organization promoting Adaptive Sports (Special Olympics Bharat; Paralympics; Deaflympics)
- Role of various professionals for children with special needs (Counsellor, Occupational Therapist, Physiotherapist, Physical Education Teacher, Speech Therapist & special Educator)

5. **YOGA**

- Meaning & Importance of Yoga
- Elements of Yoga
- Introduction - Asanas, Pranayam, Meditation & Yogic Kriyas
- Yoga for concentration & related Asanas (Sukhasana; Tadasana; Padmasana & Shashankasana, Naukasana, Vrikshasana (Tree pose), Garudasana (Eagle pose)

6. **PHYSICAL ACTIVITY & LEADERSHIP TRAINING**

- Leadership Qualities & Role of a Leader
- Meaning, objectives & types of Adventure Sports (Rock Climbing, Tracking, River Rafting, Mountaineering, Surfing and Paragliding)
- Safety measures to prevent sports injuries

9. **PSYCHOLOGY & SPORTS**

- Definition & Importance of Psychology in Phy. Edu. & Sports
- Define & Differentiate Between Growth & Development.
- Adolescent Problems & Their Management

10. **TRAINING AND DOPING IN SPORTS**

- Meaning & Concept of Sports Training
- Principles of Sports Training
- Concept & classification of doping
- Prohibited Substances & their side effects

CBSE Circular

Acad - 51/2021, 05 July 2021

Exam Scheme Term I & II

केन्द्रीय माध्यमिक शिक्षा बोर्ड
(शिक्षा मंत्रालय, भारत सरकार के अधीन एक स्वायत संगठन)
CENTRAL BOARD OF SECONDARY EDUCATION
(An Autonomous Organisation under the Ministryof Education, Govt. of India)

CBSE/DIR (ACAD)/2021

Date: July 05, 2021
Circular No: Acad-51/2021

All the Heads of Schools affiliated to CBSE

Subject: Special Scheme of Assessment for Board Examination Classes X and XII for the Session 2021-22

COVID 19 pandemic caused almost all CBSE schools to function in a virtual mode for most part of the academic session of 2020-21. Due to the extreme risk associated with the conduct of Board examinations during the second wave in April 2021, CBSE had to cancel both its class X and XII Board examinations of the year 2021 and results are to be declared on the basis of a credible, reliable, flexible and valid alternative assessment policy. This, in turn, also necessitated deliberations over alternative ways to look at the learning objectives as well as the conduct of the Board Examinations for the academic session 2021-22 in case the situation remains unfeasible.

CBSE has also held stake holder consultations with Government schools as well as private independent schools from across the country especially schools from the remote rural areas and a majority of them have requested for the rationalization of the syllabus, similar to last year in view of reduced time permitted for organizing online classes. The Board has also considered the concerns regarding differential availability of electronic gadgets, connectivity and effectiveness of online teaching and other socio-economic issues specially with respect to students from economically weaker section and those residing in far flung areas of the country. In a survey conducted by CBSE, it was revealed that the rationalized syllabus notified for the session 2020-21 was effective for schools in covering the syllabus and helped learners in achieving learning objectives in a less stressful manner.

In the above backdrop and in line with the Board's continued focus on assessing stipulated learning outcomes by making the examinations competencies and core concepts based, student-centric, transparent, technology-driven, and having advance provision of alternatives for different future scenarios, the following schemes are introduced for the Academic Session for Class X and Class XII 2021-22.

केन्द्रीय माध्यमिक शिक्षा बोर्ड

(शिक्षा मंत्रालय, भारत सरकार के अधीन एक स्वायत संगठन)

CENTRAL BOARD OF SECONDARY EDUCATION

(An Autonomous Organisation under the Ministryof Education, Govt. of India)

Special Scheme for 2021-22

A. Academic session to be divided into 2 Terms with approximately 50% syllabus in each term:

The syllabus for the Academic session 2021-22 will be divided into 2 terms by following a systematic approach by looking into the interconnectivity of concepts and topics by the Subject Experts and the Board will conduct examinations at the end of each term on the basis of the bifurcated syllabus. This is done to increase the probability of having a Board conducted classes X and XII examinations at the end of the academic session.

B. The syllabus for the Board examination 2021-22 will be rationalized similar to that of the last academic session to be notified in July 2021. For academic transactions, however, schools will follow the curriculum and syllabus released by the Board vide Circular no. F.1001/CBSE-Acad/Curriculum/2021 dated 31 March 2021. Schools will also use alternative academic calendar and inputs from the NCERT on transacting the curriculum.

C. Efforts will be made to make Internal Assessment/ Practical/ Project work more credible and valid as per the guidelines and Moderation Policy to be announced by the Board to ensure fair distribution of marks.

Details of Curriculum Transaction

- Schools will continue teaching in distance mode till the authorities permit in-person mode of teaching in schools.

- **Classes IX-X: Internal Assessment** (throughout the year-irrespective of Term I and II) would include the *3 periodic tests, student enrichment, portfolio and practical work/ speaking listening activities/ project.*

- **Classes XI-XII: Internal Assessment** (throughout the year-irrespective of Term I and II) would include end of topic or unit tests/ exploratory activities/ practicals/ projects.

- Schools would create a student profile for all assessment undertaken over the year and retain the evidences in digital format.

- CBSE will facilitate schools to upload marks of Internal Assessment on the CBSE IT platform.

- Guidelines for Internal Assessment for all subjects will also be released along with the rationalized term wise divided syllabus for the session 2021-22.The Board would also provide additional resources like sample assessments, question banks, teacher training etc. for more reliable and valid internal assessments.

केन्द्रीय माध्यमिक शिक्षा बोर्ड

(शिक्षा मंत्रालय, भारत सरकार के अधीन एक स्वायत संगठन)

CENTRAL BOARD OF SECONDARY EDUCATION

(An Autonomous Organisation under the Ministryof Education, Govt. of India)

Term I Examinations:

- At the end of the first term, the Board will organize **Term I Examination** in a flexible schedule to be conducted between November-December 2021 with a window period of 4-8 weeks for schools situated in different parts of country and abroad. Dates for conduct of examinations will be notified subsequently.

- The Question Paper will have Multiple Choice Questions (MCQ) including case-based MCQs and MCQs on assertion-reasoning type. Duration of test will be **90 minutes** and it will cover only the rationalized syllabus of **Term I only** (i.e. approx. 50% of the entire syllabus).

- Question Papers will be sent by the CBSE to schools along with marking scheme.

- The exams will be conducted under the supervision of the External Center Superintendents and Observers appointed by CBSE.

- The responses of students will be captured on OMR sheets which, after scanning may be directly uploaded at CBSE portal or alternatively may be evaluated and marks obtained will be uploaded by the school on the very same day. The final direction in this regard will be conveyed to schools by the Examination Unit of the Board.

- Marks of the **Term I** Examination will contribute to the final overall score of students.

Term II Examination/ Year-end Examination:

- At the end of the second term, the Board would organize **Term II or Year-end Examination** based on the rationalized syllabus of Term II only (i.e. approximately 50% of the entire syllabus).

- This examination would be held around **March-April 2022** at the examination centres fixed by the Board.

- The paper will be of **2 hours duration** and have questions of different formats (case-based/ situation based, open ended- short answer/ long answer type).

- In case the situation is not conducive for normal descriptive examination a **90 minute MCQ based exam** will be conducted at the end of the Term II also.

- Marks of the Term II Examination would contribute to the final overall score.

केन्द्रीय माध्यमिक शिक्षा बोर्ड
(शिक्षा मंत्रालय, भारत सरकार के अधीन एक स्वायत संगठन)

CENTRAL BOARD OF SECONDARY EDUCATION
(An Autonomous Organisation under the Ministryof Education, Govt. of India)

<u>Assessment / Examination as per different situations</u>

A. In case the situation of the pandemic improves and students are able to come to schools or centres for taking the exams.

Board would conduct Term I and Term II examinations at schools/centres and the theory marks will be distributed equally between the two exams.

B. In case the situation of the pandemic forces complete closure of schools during November-December 2021, but Term II exams are held at schools or centres.

Term I MCQ based examination would be done by students online/offline from home - in this case, the weightage of this exam for the final score would be reduced, and weightage of Term II exams will be increased for declaration of final result.

C. In case the situation of the pandemic forces complete closure of schools during March-April 2022, but Term I exams are held at schools or centres.

Results would be based on the performance of students on Term I MCQ based examination and internal assessments. The weightage of marks of Term I examination conducted by the Board will be increased to provide year end results of candidates.

D. In case the situation of the pandemic forces complete closure of schools and Board conducted Term I and II exams are taken by the candidates from home in the session 2021-22.

Results would be computed on the basis of the Internal Assessment/Practical/Project Work and Theory marks of Term-I and II exams taken by the candidate from home in Class X / XII subject to the moderation or other measures to ensure validity and reliability of the assessment.

In all the above cases, data analysis of marks of students will be undertaken to ensure the integrity of internal assessments and home based exams.

Dr. Joseph Emmanuel
Director (Academics)

CHAPTER 01

Physical Education and Sports for CWSN

(Children with Special Needs: Divyang)

In this Chapter...

- Adaptive Physical Education
- Adaptive Sports
- Organisations Promoting Adaptive Sports
- Role of Professionals for Children with Special Needs

Today, even physically challenged people (Divyang) have the opportunity to participate in all physical education events with full enthusiasm. The education programme that enables them to do so is called adaptive physical education.

Such an education includes various special education teachers who train children with disabilities to participate in various local, state, national, and even international sports events such as Special Olympics, Paralympics, Deaflympics, etc.

Adaptive Physical Education

Adaptive physical education programmes are school based programmes for children with disabilities like deafness/hearing impairment, blindness, speech impairment, any type of physical impairments, autism, mental retardation etc.

Children with disabilities have special needs because they are not able to participate in regular physical exercises and activities. So the adapted physical education programme is specially designed for individuals with disabilities.

It can be defined as, "Adapted physical education is the art and science of developing, implementing and monitoring a carefully designed physical education instructional programme for learners with disabilities."

In other words, it is a diversified programme which includes developmental activities, games, sports, etc, that suit the interests, capacities and limitation of children with disabilities.

It is a sub disciple of physical education that focuses on the creation of individualised programmes for students who may safely or successfully engage in unrestricted participation in physical education programmes.

Adaptive physical education provides safe, personally satisfying and successful experiences of physical ability to children who are differently abled.

Adaptive physical education programmes focus on the development of composition, posture, balance, coordination motor skills, etc. It teaches modified and suitable alternative activities which are more helpful in different circumstances.

Aims of Adaptive Physical Education

The aim of an adaptive physical education programme is as follows

- Providing physical education that meets the unique needs of such children.
- Development of the student's motor skills.
- To assist differently abled students in achieving mental, emotional, physical and social growth.

- Achieving meaningful success and positive education outcomes.
- Developing self-esteem and improving socialisation skills.
- Coping with disabilities through an active and healthy lifestyle.
- Developing cognitive abilities to improve education results.

Objectives of Adaptive Physical Education

The objectives are discussed as follows

1. **To Develop Motor Skills** According to this objective, the emphasis is onto develop motor skills of students with disabilities. Motor skills are necessary for performing not only specific skills but daily routine activities also. These skills enable physically disabled students to be active and smart.

2. **To Improve Physical Fitness** It is an important objective of adaptive physical education in which modified or adaptive exercises are provided in the programmes to improve physical fitness of students.

3. **To Ensure Students Participation in Physical Education Programmes** This objective focuses on ensuring that each students actively participates in physical education programmes regularly. It also ensures that the student is integrated into regular education programme whenever possible.

4. **To Promote Sportsmanship Qualities** It is another vital objective of adaptive physical education to promote sportsmanship qualities among the differently abled students. Participation in adaptive physical education programmes naturally improves sportsman qualities.

5. **To Ensure Services to Differently Abled Students** This objective ensures that the differently abled students are provided with the physical education services that meet their special needs properly.

6. **To Improve Social Adjustments** Participation in programmes of adaptive physical education helps the differently abled students to make social adjustments, as such adjustments are most important especially in present day society.

Overall, the aims and objectives of adapted physical education programmes is to make the children with special needs cope with their disabilities in a better way.

Adaptive Sports

Adaptive sports are the type of competitive sports that are designed for individuals with disabilities. These sports are slightly different than normal sports as there may be some modifications in the rules or in the equipment to meet the special needs of the participants. For instance, sled hockey allows the use of sleds for players to sit and play the game.

Organisations Promoting Adaptive Sports

For the promotion and organisation of adaptive sports, many different competitions are held. Some of them are **Special Olympics Bharat**, **Paralympics**, **Deaflympics** etc.

These competitions provide a good platform for individuals with disabilities to participate.

Special Olympics Bharat

Special Olympics Bharat is a National Sports Federation in India accredited by Special Olympics International that uses sports as a catalyst to transform the lives of children and people with intellectual disabilities like Down Syndrome, Autism, ADHD and others.

It was founded in 1987 as 'Special Olympics India' and later the name was changed to 'Special Olympics Bharat' in 2001. It is registered under the Indian Trusts Act, 1882 (amended in 2015). It is recognised by the Government of India as a National Sports Federation in priority category. It works for development of sports opportunity for the people with intellectual disabilities.

It is officially recognised programme of Special Olympics International founded by Eunice Kennedy. It is a designated Nodal Agency for all disabilities.

Vision

Its vision is to inspire children and people with intellectual disabilities to take up games and sports so that there is a general acceptance and inclusion of these people in society.

Special Olympics Bharat strives to

- Focus on holistic development and training that goes beyond the classrooms into the playing fields, etc, to encourage children with disabilities to join and remain in school.
- Create role models with a view to inspire the children and also motivate parents to send their children to school and to participate in sports and other extra-curricular activities.
- Train teachers to sensitise them to needs of special children, and create a cadre of physical education teachers from among the disabled who can work with schools and community centers.
- Ensure maximum involvement of community for greater public understanding and acceptance of people with intellectual disabilities.

Mission

Its mission is to provide adequate sports infrastructure and training to develop fitness, courage, confidence, good health, joy etc. for children and adults with intellectual disabilities.

It also focuses on making them participate in sharing of gifts, skills and friendship with their family, friends and the community.

Oath

The oath of Special Olympics Bharat is *"Let me win, but if I cannot win, let me be brave in the attempt."*

Benefits of Special Olympic Bharat

- It is helpful in developing a positive attitude, self-confidence and self-worth.
- It improves motor skills and physical fitness.
- It promotes mental, physical, social and emotional development.
- It increases family support and social acceptance.

Organisation of Sports Championship

Special Olympics Bharat organises championships at local, district, state, national and international level like National Games, National Football, Table Tennis Championship, National Floor Hockey Championship, National Volleyball, National Badminton Championship, etc. It has sent a number of athletes for summer and winter international sports events.

Paralympics

Paralympics is derived from the Greek word which means 'parallel to Olympics'. **Dr Ludwig Guttmann** is credited with the starting of the paralympic movement which is an Olympic event for physically and intellectually disabled persons.

Guttmann was a neurologist during World War II and treated British War casualties. He founded the National Spinal Injuries Centre at Stoke Mandeville Hospital in England.

In July 1948, Guttmann organised a sports competition for British World War II patients with spinal cord injuries.

This event was hugely popular and in 1960 after the Rome Olympics, **Paralympic events were held for the first time** in Rome. Since then, these games are held at an interval of every four years following the Olympic games.

Paralympic Logo

International Paralympic Committee

This committee was founded on 22nd September, 1989. It organises Paralympics after every four years in the same year in which Olympics are held.

After every Summer and Winter Olympics, Summer Paralympic and Winter Paralympics are held at the same venue.

The International Paralympic Committe also serve as the International Federation for nine sports, for which it supervises and coordinates the world championship and other competitions. Its headquater is located in Bonn, Germany.

The aim of IPC is to develop sports opportunities for all the people with an impairment from the beginner to the elite level.

The Paralympic Committee has allowed competitions in ten eligible impairment types. They are

1. Impaired muscle power
2. Impaired passive range of movements
3. Loss of limb
4. Leg length difference
5. Short stature
6. Hypertonia (*i.e.* spastics)
7. Ataxia (lack of muscle coordination)
8. Athetosis (a brain disorder causing involuntary writhing movements)
9. Vision impairment (*i.e.* blindness)
10. Intellectual impairment

Deaflympics

Deaflympics is an international Olympic event at which deaf athletes compete. Unlike other paralympic events, deaf athletes cannot be guided by sounds like referee whistle, gunshot etc. Therefore, special arrangements are made for the deaf athletes at Deaflympics such as waving a flag, using light instead of gunshots etc.

The Deaflympics are more than just the world's second oldest multiple sports after olympics. These games are the world's fastest growing sports events.

The Deaflympics are an equivalent to the Olympic games for deaf athletes. These games have been organised by the International Committee of sports for deaf since the first event.

The first of such games were held in Paris in 1924. Since then, these games have been held regularly after every four years. The Deaflympics Winter Games were started in 1949.

From 1924 to 1965, these games were officially known as the 'International Games for the Deaf' or the 'International Silent Games'.

From 1966 to 1999, they were recognised as 'World Games for the Deaf' or the 'World Silent Games'.

Since 2001, these games are renamed as Deaflympics'. Till now, the Deaflympics have been hosted by 36 cities in 21 countries.

Motto and Logo

The Motto of Deaflympics is *'Per Ludos Aequalitas'* meaning *'Equality through sports'*. It's logo is inspired by the sign for Olympics. The circle in the middle represents an eye because deaf people have more visual power.

The four colours of the logo *i.e.* **red**, **green**, **yellow** and **blue** represent the four regional confederations of the International Committee of Sports for Deaf *viz.* Europe, Asia Pacific, Pan-America and Africa. It ties together the strong elements, sign language, deaf and international cultures, unity and continuity.

Deaflympics Logo

Objective

The main purpose of Deaflympics is to provide opportunities to person with hearing disability to participate in elite sports.

Eligibility Criteria

The eligibility criteria to compete at the Deaflympic Games, the athletes must have a hearing loss of minimum 55 decibel in their better ear. Hearing aid, cochlear implants, etc., are not allowed to be used in the competition.

Summer and Winter Deaflympics

The sports included in Summer Deaflympics are Athletics, Badminton, Basketball, Beach Volleyball, Bowling, Cycling Road, Football, Handball, Judo, Shooting, Karate, Orienteering, Swimming, Table Tennis, etc.

The sports that are included in Winter Deaflympics are Alpine skiing, Cross-country skiing, Curling, Ice Hockey, and Snowboard.

Year and Venue of Summer Deaflympics

S. No.	Year	City	Country
I	1924	Paris	France
II	1928	Amsterdam	Netherlands
III	1931	Nuremberg	Germany
IV	1935	London	Great Britain
V	1939	Stockholm	Sweden
VI	1949	Copenhagen	Denmark
VII	1953	Brussels	Belgium
VIII	1957	Milan	Italy
IX	1961	Helsinki	Finland
X	1965	Washington DC	United States
XI	1969	Belgrade	Yugoslavia
XII	1973	Malmo	Sweden
XIII	1977	Bucharest	Romania
XIV	1981	Cologne	West Germany
XV	1985	Los Angeles	United States
XVI	1989	Christchurch	New Zealand
XVII	1993	Sofia	Bulgaria
XVIII	1997	Copenhagen	Denmark
XIX	2001	Rome	Italy
XX	2005	Melbourne	Australia
XXI	2009	Taipei	Chinese Taipei
XXII	2013	Sofia	Bulgaria
XXIII	2017	Samsun	Turkey
XXIV	2022	Caxias do sul	Brazil

Year and Venue of Winter Deaflympics

S. No.	Year	City	Country
I	1949	Seefeld	Austria
II	1953	Oslo	Norway
III	1955	Oberammergaau	Germany
IV	1959	Montana-Vennala	Switzerland
V	1963	Are	Sweden
VI	1967	Berchtesgaden	West Germany
VII	1971	Adelboden	Switzerland
VIII	1975	Lake Placid	United States
IX	1979	Meribel	France

S. No.	Year	City	Country
X	1983	Madonna di Campiglio	Italy
XI	1987	Oslo	Norway
XII	1991	Banff	Canada
XIII	1995	Yllas	Finland
XIV	1999	Davos	Switzerland
XV	2003	Sundsvall	Sweden
XVI	2007	Salt Lake City	United States
XVII	2015	Khanty-Mansiyak	Russia
XVIII	2019	Sondrio Province	Italy
XIX	2023	Quebec	Canada

Role of Professionals for Children with Special Needs

The professionals who work with children with special needs have to focus on their overall development. They help and support such children in achieving their full potential, giving ability to communicate properly, etc.

The professionals working with these children are counsellors, occupational therapists, physiotherapists, physical education teachers, speech therapists and special educators.

The roles of these professionals are discussed below

Counsellor

A counsellor is a trusted professional who provides a safe and supportive environment. The role of the counsellor is to discuss the concerns of the child with special needs and understand the feelings, emotions and sentiments of the child.

A counsellor also counsels the parents, guardians and teachers of the child with special needs. He provides guidance and helps the child to adapt to different situations because he understands the mental and physical needs of the child.

A counsellor helps students with special needs with their academic goals, their social, personal and career development.

He also carries out various development programmes related to stress management, anger management, conflict management, positive thinking, etc. He provides social support to the child along with exploring ways to make the disability more manageable. A counsellor helps the child to cope better with the disability.

Occupational Therapist

An occupational therapist is a professional who helps the children with special needs to develop fine and gross motor skills like eating, dressing, bathing, drinking etc.

An occupational therapist also helps them develop their sensory and cognitive abilities. This is done by teaching simple activities like grasping, reaching, picking, dressing, feeding etc.

The primary aim of an occupational therapist is to maximise the child's potential to participate in activities of everyday life by minimising the impact of their disability.

The role of an occupational therapist is to develop physical coordination among the children with special needs like hand-eye coordination to improve skills such as hitting a ball or copying from a blackboard, etc. This professional also arranges for any specialised equipment if required by the child.

Physiotherapist

The role of the physiotherapist is to manage children with movement disorders. He teaches them how to balance their movements while walking, rolling, sitting and crawling. For this, various exercises are taught that also prevent the development of deformities.

Another role of the physiotherapist is to encourage a child's independence and mobility, thereby helping in building self-esteem. He evaluates movements and functions of the body with special reference to physical mobility, balance, posture, gain, fatigue, etc. He uses range of techniques like massage, exercise, electrotheraphy and hydrotheraphy, etc.

A physiotherapist also identifies the type of equipment that can help a child in managing movement disorders.

Physical Education Teacher

Physical education teacher generally determines the abilities of students with special needs and also the procedures that may need to be implemented to support their participation in sports and physical fitness.

The physical education teachers help students with special needs to improve their physical fitness. They help in improving hand-eye coordination, flexibility, muscular strength, endurance and even cardiovascular efficiency of students with special needs.

The physical education teachers also teach physical activities which may help in reducing stress tension, depression and anxiety of the students with special needs.

They also help students with special needs in developing a feeling of self-esteem and social awareness as the students with special needs may often feel isolated and removed from the group. They organise various physical activities for students with special needs to promote their mental and physical health.

Speech Therapist

The role of a speech therapist is to build the communication of children with special needs. This is done by teaching them how to use words, sounds of speech, gestures and maintenance of eye contact.

His essential job is to help the children to express themselves using oral communication skills or sounds and gestures. This helps in emotional development as well as building confidence in children with special needs.

Speech therapist also helps such students who have fluency disorders like stoppages, repetitions or prolonging sounds in words, etc.

Special Educator

The role of a special educator is to work for the overall development of children with special needs. This is done by developing teaching aids and instructional materials as well as through remedial teaching.

Special educators are concerned with the overall success of children with special needs. Their role is to improve a student's ability to function in social, emotional and behavioural capacities.

Another role of special educator is to encourage family involvement, working with other school staff to better understand the needs of the specific child, etc. For this purpose, collaborating with school and community professionals is also required.

Chapter Practice

PART 1

Objective Questions

• Multiple Choice Questions

1. The aim of adaptive physical education is to help whom?

(a) Adults   (b) Differently abled students
(c) Athelets   (d) All of these

Ans. (b) The aim of adaptive physical education is to help differently abled students. It develops the opportunity for the differently abled students to participate in physical activity.

2. Which of the following organisations helps promoting adaptive sports?

(a) Special Olympics Bharat (b) Deaflympics
(c) Paralympics   (d) All of the above

Ans. (d) All the given such as Special Olympics Bharat, Deaflympics and Paralympics help in promoting adaptive sports.

3. In which year, the name of 'Special Olympics India' was changed to 'Special Bharat Olympics' ?

(a) 1985   (b) 2000
(c) 2001   (d) 2002

Ans. (c) In the year 2001, the name was changed to Special Olympics Bharat from Special Olympics India.

4. In which year the International Paralympic Committee was founded?

(a) 22nd September, 1989   (b) 22nd September, 1990
(c) 20th September, 1989   (d) 20th September, 1992

Ans. (a) International Paralympic Committee was founded on 22nd September, 1989 to organise paralympics after every four years.

5. How many types of competition has been allowed by the paralympic committee?

(a) 12   (b) 10   (c) 15   (d) 22

Ans. (b) A total of 10 types of competitions are allowed by the paralympics committee.

6. Identify the event for which this logo is

(a) Summer Olympics
(b) Paralympics
(c) Winter Olympics
(d) International Cricket Council

Ans. (b) The logo is for Paralympics. The event supports leadership, promotes health and develops confidence.

7. The given logo is used for sports event organised in India. Name it

(a) Special Olympics Bharat
(b) Cerebral Palsy Games
(c) Para Sports
(d) Wheelchair Racing

Ans. (a) The given logo is for a specific sports event 'Special Olympic Bharat' which is organised for differently abled people.

8. Match the following.

List I (Summer Deaflympics, Host City)	List II (Year)
A. Nuremberg	1. 1953
B. Brussels	2. 2005
C. Melbourne	3. 1997
D. Copenhagen	4. 1931

Codes

	A	B	C	D			A	B	C	D
(a)	1	2	3	4		(b)	4	1	2	3
(c)	2	3	4	1		(d)	3	4	1	2

Ans. (b) The options in the left are the names of the cities where summer deaflympics were held. On the right column are the year in which the events were held. So Nuremberg hosts the event in 1931, Brussels in 1953, Melbourne in 2005 and Copenhagen in 1997.

9. Match the following.

List I (Adaptive Sports)		List II (Year of Starting
A. Special Olympics Bharat	1.	1989
B. International Paralympics Committee	2.	1949
C. Deaflympic Winter Games	3.	1987

Codes

	A	B	C			A	B	C
(a)	3	1	2	(b)		1	3	2
(c)	2	1	3	(d)		3	2	1

Ans. (a) The left column indicates the organisations promoting adaptive sports and the right column indicates the years in which these organisations were formed. Special Olympic Bharat was formed in 1987, International Paralympics Committee was formed in 1989 and Deaflympics Winter Games were held in 1949 for the first time.

10. Match the following.

List I		List II
A. Counsellor	1.	Overall development of CWSN
B. Physiotherapist	2.	Understand feelings of CWSN
C. Special educator	3.	Oral Communication Skills
D. Speech therapist	4.	Manage Movement disorders

Codes

	A	B	C	D			A	B	C	D
(a)	1	3	2	4	(b)		4	1	3	2
(c)	2	4	1	3	(d)		2	1	3	4

Ans. (c) The left column indicates the professionals and the right column indicates the work. Counsellor understands the feeling of CWSN. Physiotherapist helps CWSN in managing movement disorders. Special educator work for overall development of CWSN and speech therapist develops oral communication skills of children facing speech problems.

11. Paralympic Games are the world's largest sporting event for the people with physical, visual and intellectual disabilities. It is held in two categories, one is Summer Olympics and the other is Winter Olympics.

Where were the first Paralympic Games held?

(a) Greece
(b) Rome
(c) New Delhi
(d) London

Ans. (b) The first Paralympics games were held in Rome in 1960 and the event became hugely popular.

12. Seetha who is studying in class XI at Kaveri Public School has a tendency to forget things along with a flickering mind. She is also not able to sit quietly in a place for a while. The teacher observed her and advised Seetha's parents during a parent teacher meeting to see a professional for CWSN.

Which among the following professional should Seetha's parents meet?

(a) Psychologist
(b) Speech therapist
(c) Physical education teacher
(d) Counsellor

Ans. (d) Seetha is facing emotional problems. Her parents should meet a counsellor to understand the feelings, emotions and sentiments of the child.

13. Raman is five year old boy facing movement disorders. He is not able to balance himself properly while walking, rolling or sitting. He should be taken to which of the following professional?

(a) Counsellor
(b) Physiotherapist
(c) Special educator
(d) Psychologist

Ans. (b) Raman is facing problems of balancing himself while walking, rolling, sitting etc. So he should be taken to a physiotherapist so that proper equipments to manage the movements can be identified.

14. These games are major international multi-sport events for the athletes with various disabilities such as mobility disabilities, blindness, cerebral palsy. Which games are discussed here?

(a) Olympics
(b) Special Olympic Bharat
(c) Paralympics
(d) Deaflympics

Ans. (c) The games discussed here is Paralympics which is a sporting event for differently abled people.

• Assertion-Reasoning MCQs

Directions (Q. Nos. 1-4) *Each of these questions contains two statements, Assertion (A) and Reason (R). Each of these questions also has four alternative choices, any one of which is the correct answer. You have to select one of the codes (a), (b), (c) and (d) given below.*

(a) Both A and R are true and R is the correct explanation of A
(b) Both A and R are true, but R is not the correct explanation of A
(c) A is true, but R is false
(d) A is false, but R is true

1. Assertion (A) Children with disabilities have special needs.

Reason (R) These children are not able to participate in regular physical exercises and activities.

Ans. (a) The Assertion is true as children with disabilities are different than normal children, so they have special needs.

The Reason is also true as due to disabilities that cannot participate in regular exercises as normal students.

So, both A and R are true and R is the correct explanation of A.

2. Assertion (A) Adaptive sports are designed for all the individuals.

Reason (R) Deaflympics is an example of the adaptive sports.

Ans. (d) Adaptive sports are designed for children and adults with disabilities and not for everyone so assertion is false.

Reason is true as deaflympics is a sporting event for the deaf people and it is part of adaptive sports.

3. Assertion (A) The motto of Deaflympics is 'Equality through sports'.

Reason (R) The role of counsellor is to manage children with movements disorder.

Ans. (c) Assertion is true as Deaflympics was formed to spread the word of equality for all irrespective of their disabilities.

Reason is false as the role of a counsellor is to provide a supportive environment and understand the feelings, emotions and sentiments of a child.

4. Assertion (A) Differently abled students should be treated equally.

Reason (R) Differently abled students should not be looked sympathetically rather they should be recognised for their talent and capabilites.

Ans. (a) The Assertion is true as differently abled students have same emotions, feelings, hope and ambitions, so they should be treated equally.

The reason is also true as differently abled students should be treated with respect. Their talents and capabilities should be recognised so that they develop self confidence. So, both A and R are true and R is the correct explanation of A.

• Case Based MCQs

1. Vishal is having intellectual impairment but he is good in sports. He wants to take part in one of the sports events that are specially developed for such people. Based on this case, answer the following

(i) Vishal can take part in _______.
(a) Deaflympics   (b) Paralympics
(c) T20 World Cup   (d) Olympic Games

Ans. (b) Vishal can take part in paralympics as he is having intellectual impairment and there are competitions for such people in paralympics.

(ii) How vishal is different from other people?
(a) He has problems of general mental ability
(b) He can see partially only
(c) He is not having one of the limbs
(d) None of the above

Ans. (a) Vishal is different from other people as he has intellectual impairment which means general mental ability problems or mental retardation.

(iii) How can physical education and sports help Vishal?
(a) Develop motor skills
(b) Improve social adjustment
(c) Improves physical fitness
(d) All of the above

Ans. (d) Physical education and sports help Vishal by developing his motor skills, improving social adjustment and physical fitness.

2. Adaptive physical education programmes focus on the development of composition, posture, balance, coordination, motor skills etc. It teaches modified and suitable alternative activities which are more helpful in different circumstances. Based on this passage, answer the following questions.

(i) Adaptive physical education programmes are meant for which of the following?
(a) Divyang   (b) Retarded
(c) Blind   (d) All of these

Ans. (d) Adaptive physical education programmes are meant for children and adults with special needs so divyang, retarded and blind, all the categories will be there.

(ii) Which of the following is an example of adaptive sports?
(a) Indian super league
(b) Special Olympics Bharat
(c) Asian Games
(d) Euro Championships

Ans. (b) Special Olympics Bharat is an example of adaptive sports that organises sports events for people with special needs or Divyang.

(iii) In adaptive sports, the sports equipments are _______.
(a) modified   (b) not used
(c) minimal   (d) All of these

Ans. (a) The sports equipments in adaptive sports are modified so that people with disabilities can practice on them.

Subjective Questions

• Short Answer (SA) Type Questions

1. Explain the adaptive physical education programme.

Ans. The adaptive physical education programme is a school based programme for children with disabilities.

Children with special needs like deafness/ hearing impairment, blindness, speech impairment, autism, mental retardation etc. are not able to participate in regular physical exercises and activities.

The adaptive physical education programme is not only for differently abled but also for the people of all ages.

The adaptive physical education programme focuses on the development of composition, posture, balance, coordination, motor skills, etc.

The programme teaches modified and suitable alternative activities which are more helpful in different circumstances.

2. What is the need for adaptive sports?

Ans. Adaptive sports are needed for the following reasons

- To enhance the self esteem and boost self confidence of children with disabilities.
- To develop social skills in such children so that they interact with normal children freely.
- To develop a sense of achievement by participating in adaptive sports and games.
- To improve their emotional skills so that they donot feel left out in the society.
- To enhance the efficiency and growth of disabled people in physical education and sports.

3. What is the aim of Adaptive Physical Education?

Ans. The aim of adaptive physical education is as follows

- Providing physical education that meets the unique needs of such children.
- Development of the student's motor skills.
- To assist differently abled students in achieving mental, emotional, physical and social growth.
- Achieving meaningful success and positive education outcomes.
- Developing self esteem and improving socialisation skills.
- Coping with disabilities through an active and healthy lifestyle.
- Developing cognitive abilities to improve education results.

4. Define Special Olympic Bharat. List the benefits of Special Olympics Bharat.

Ans. Special Olympics Bharat is a government organisation made for the development of sports opportunity for the people with intellectual disabilities.

It was founded in 1987 as special Olympics India and later the name was changed to special Olympic Bharat in 2001. It is officially recognised programme of Special Olympics International founded by Eunice kennedy. It is a designated Nodal Agency for all disabilities.

Benefits of Special Olympic Bharat are as follows

- It is helpful in developing a positive attitude, self-confidence and self-worth.
- It improves motor skills and physical fitness.
- It promotes mental, physical, social and emotional development.
- It increases family support and social acceptance.

5. What is the vision and mission of Special Olympics Bharat?

Ans. Vision of special Olympic Bharat is to inspire children and people with intellectual disabilities to take up games and sports so that there is a general acceptance and inclusion of these people in society. Mission of special Olympic Bharat is provide adequate sports infrastructure and training to develops fitness, courage, confidence, good health, joy etc. for children and adults with intellectual disabilities.

6. Mention three objectives of Special Olympics Bharat.

Ans. The objectives of Special Olympics Bharat are as follows

- Focus on holistic development and training that goes beyond the classrooms into the playing fields, etc, to encourage children with disabilities to join and remain in school.
- Create role models with a view to inspire the children and also motivate parents to send their children to school and to participate in sports and other extra-curricular activities.
- Train teachers to sensitise them to needs of special children and create a cadre of physical education teachers from among the disabled who can work with schools and community centers.

7. When was the International Paralympic Committee formed? What are the categories of impairment eligible to take part in it?

Ans. International Paralympic Committee was formed on 22nd September, 1989.

The Paralympic Committee has allowed competitions in ten eligible impairment types.

These are as follows

1. Impaired muscle power.
2. Impaired passive range of movements.
3. Loss of limb.
4. Leg length difference.
5. Short stature.
6. Hypertonia (i.e. spastics)
7. Ataxia (lack of muscle coordination)
8. Athetosis (a brain disorder causing involuntary writhing movements).
9. Vision impairment (i.e. blindness).
10. Intellectual impairment.

8. Write a short note on how Paralympics started?

Ans. Paralympics was started due to the efforts of Dr Ludwig Guttmann. He was a neurologist who treated British war casualties during World War II. He founded the National Spinal Injuries Centre at Stoke Mandeville Hospital in England.

Then in July 1948, Guttmann organised a sports competition for patients with spinal cord injuries which became immensely popular. This was the first event of this type after which the Paralympics were held regularly after every four years.

Paralympics events were held the first time in Rome.

9. What is Deaflympics and discuss the eligibility criteria to compete at Deaflympics? Which sports are included in Summer Deaflympics?

Ans. Deaflympics is an international Olympic event at which deaf athletes compete. Unlike other paralympic events, deaf athletes cannot be guided by sounds like referee whisstle, gunshot etc. Some special arrangements are made for them like waving a flag, using light instead of gunshot etc. The eligibility criteria to compete at Deaflympic Games, the athletes must have a hearing loss of minimum 55 decibel in their better ear. Hearing aid, cochlear implants etc. are not allowed to be used in the competition.

The sports included in Summer Deaflympics are Athletics, Badminton, Basketball, Beach Volleyball, Bowling, Cycling, Football, Handball, Judo, Shooting, Karate, Orienteering, Swimming, Table Tennis, etc.

10. Explain the role of a counsellor in developing a supportive environment for children with special needs.

Ans. The role of a counsellor is to develop a safe and supportive environment for children with special needs. He does this by understanding the feelings, emotions and sentiments of the child.

The counsellor counsels the child's parents, guardians and teachers on how to deal with different situations related to the child. The counsellor also develops social support for the child so that the child could manage his/her disability in a better way.

A counsellor also comes out with developmental programmes related to stress management.

So, a counsellor guides the child, its parents and society in developing a supportive environment.

11. How can an occupational therapist help a child with special needs?

Ans. An occupational therapist is a professional who can help a child with special needs by developing its fine and gross motor skills. The primary aim of an occupational therapist is to maximise the child's potential to participate in activities of everyday life by minimising the impact of their Disability. This is done by teaching simple activities like grasping, reaching, picking, dressing etc.

These activities increase physical coordination among such children. When the child is able to do simple activities independently, it builds confidence in the child. The occupational therapist also arranges for any special equipment needed by the child.

12. Differentiate between counsellor and physiotherapist on the basis of their work.

Ans. The differences between counsellor and physiotherapist are as follows

Counsellor	Physiotherapist
The role of the counsellor is to discuss the concerns of the child with special needs and understand the feelings, emotions and sentiments of the child.	The role of the physiotherapist is to manage children with movement disorder. He teaches them how to balance their movement while walking, sitting etc.
A counsellor also counsels the parents, guardians and teachers of the child with special needs.	Physiotherapist evaluates movements and functions of the body with special reference to physical mobility, balance, posture etc.

13. What is the role of physical educator in dealing with CWSN?

Ans. The role of physical education teacher is to generally determines the abilities of students with special needs and also the procedures that may need to be implemented to support their participation in sports and physical fitness.

The physical education teachers help students with special needs to improve their physical fitness. They help in improving hand-eye coordination, flexibility, muscular strength, endurance and even cardiovascular efficiency of students with special needs.

The physical education teachers also teach physical activities which may help in reducing stress, tension, depression and anxiety of the students with special needs.

They also help students with special needs in developing a feeling of self-esteem and social awarness as the students with special needs may often feel isolated and removed from the group.

14. How a Speech Therapist can help the children cope up with speech difficulties?

Ans. Speech therapist can help the children to copeup with speech difficulties as he build the communication to the children facing speech difficulties. This is done by teaching them how to use words, sounds of speech, gestures and maintenance of eye contact.

His essential job is to help the children to express themselves using oral communication skills or sounds and gestures. This helps in emotional development as well as building confidence in children with special needs.

Speech therapist also helps such students who have fluency disorders like stoppages, repetitions or prolonging sounds in words, etc.

• Long Answer (LA) Type Questions

1. Enumerate the objectives of adaptive physical education.

Ans. The objectives of adaptive physical education are as follows

(i) **To Develop Motor Skills** This objective emphasis on developing motor skills of students with disabilities. They are necessary for performing not only specific skills but daily routine activities.

(ii) **To Improve Physical Fitness** This objective is to provide modified or adaptive exercises to students in order to improve their physical fitness.

(iii) **To Ensure Students Participation in Physical Education Programmes** This objective ensure that each student actively participate in physical education programmes regularly at his/her own level.

(iv) **To Promote Sportsmanship Qualities** This objective ensures promotion of sportsmanship qualities among differently abled students.

(v) **To Ensure Services to Differently Abled Students** This objective ensures that the differently abled students are provided with proper services that meet their needs.

(vi) **To Improve Social Adjustments** This objective is essential especially in present day world as the participation in programmes of adaptive physical education helps differently abled students to make social adjustments.

2. Explain in detail about how Paralympics was formed?

Ans. 'Paralympics' is derived from the Greek word which means 'parallel to Olympics'. Dr Ludwig Guttmann is credited with the starting of the paralympic movement which is an Olympic event for physically and intellectually disabled persons.

Guttmann was a neurologist during World War II and treated British War casualties. He founded the National Spinal Injuries Centre at Stoke Mandeville Hospital in England.

In July 1948, Guttmann organised a sports competition for British World War II patients with spinal cord injuries.

This event war hugely popular and in 1960 after the Rome Olympics, Paralympic events were held for the first time in Rome. Since then, these games are held at an interval of every four years following the Olympic Games.

Seeing the rising popularity of the sports events International Paralympic Committee was formed.

This committee was founded on 22nd September, 1989. It organises Paralympics after every four years in the same year in which Olympics are held.

After every Summer and Winter Olympics, Summer Paralympic and Winter Paralympics are held at the same venue.

The International Paralympic Committee also serve as the International Federation for nine sports, for which it supervises and coordinates the world championship and other competitions. Its headquater is located in Bonn, Germany.

3. Disuss about 'Deaflympics' in detail.

Ans. Deaflympics are the world's second oldest multiple sports after Olympics. The Deaflym pics is an International Olympic Committee sanctioned event at which deaf athletes compete at an international level. The Deaflympics games are held after every four years.

The first Deaflympics Games were held in Paris in 1924. In that deaflympics, only 148 deaf athletes from nine European countries participated.

From 1924-1965, these games were officially known as the 'International Games for the Deaf'. From 1966-1999, they were called 'World Games for the Deaf'. Since, 2001, these games are known as 'Deaflympics'.

In Deaflympics the starter's gun bullhorn commands or refree's whistles are not used, rather flags or any visual signals are used to alert participants.

The motto of Deaflympics is 'Equality through sports'. The four colours of the logo i.e. red, green, yellow and blue, represent the four regional confederations of the International Committee of Sports for the Deaf viz. Europe, Asia Pacific, Pan-America and Africa. The circle in the middle represents an eye as deaf people are very visual. The athletes, to compete in Deaflympics, must have a hearing loss of minimum 55 decible in their better ear.

So, it can be said the Deaflympics provide ample opportunities to persons with hearing disability to participates in sports competitions.

4. What is the role of professionals who work for children with special needs. Explain the role of any one professional.

Ans. The professionals who work with children with special needs have to focus on their overall development. They help and support such children in achieving their full potential, giving ability to communicate properly, etc. Their role is to understand the specific need of CWSN and devise pragrammes, activities and games accordingly.

The professionals working with these children are counsellors, occupational therapists, physiotherapists, physical education teachers, speech therapists and special educators.

The role of a Counsellor is as follows

A counsellor is a trusted professional who provides a safe and supportive environment. The role of the counsellor is to discuss the concerns of the child with special needs and understand the feelings, emotions and sentiments of the child.

A counsellor also counsels the parents, guardians and teachers of the child with special needs. He provides guidance and helps the child to adapt to different situations because he understands the mental and physical needs of the child.

A counsellor helps students with special needs with their academic goals, their social, personal and career development.

He also carries out various development programmes related to stress management, anger management, conflict management, positive thinking, etc.

He provides social support to the child along with exploring ways to make the disability more manageable. A counsellor helps the child to cope better with the disability.

• Case Based Questions

1. Children with special needs have to cope up with many kinds of problems. Some professionals teach the children how to use words, sounds of speech, gestures and maintenance of eye contact. The objective is to help the children to express themselves using oral communication skills.

(i) Which professions are specially designated to work for children with special needs?

Ans. Professions like counsellor, occupational therapist, physiotherapist, physical education teacher, speech therapist and special educator work for children with special needs.

(ii) What is the role of a speech therapist for children with special needs?

Ans. The role of a speech therapist is to build the communication of children with special needs by teaching them the use of words, sounds, gestures etc to express themselves.

2. Prabha is a Divyang. She is in 9th standard and likes to take part in sports activities. Her younger sister also takes part in sports. But the equipments used by Prabha for playing is different than what her sister uses. Based on this case answer the following.

(i) Why Prabha's equipments are different from her sisters?

Ans. Prabhas equipments are different from her sister because they are specifically designed for the children with special needs to play adaptive sports.

(ii) How physical education help CWSN?

Ans. Physical education provide and develop need based programmes for children with disabilities.

3. Special Olympics Bharat organises championships at local, district, state, national and international level like National Games, National Football, Table Tennis Championship, National Floor Hockey Championship, National Volleyball, National Badminton Championship, etc. It has sent a number of athletes for world summer and winter games.

(i) Why Special Olympics Bharat was formed?

Ans. It was formed to provide sports opportunity to people with intellectual and physical disabilities.

(ii) What is the vision of Special Olympics Bharat?

Ans. The vision is to inspire children and people with intellectual disabilities to take up games and sports so that there is general acceptance and inclusion of these people in society.

Chapter Test

Multiple Choice Questions

1. Special Olympics Bharat organises championships at which level(s)?

(a) Local level   (b) State level   (c) International level   (d) All of these

2. Which country hosted Summer Deaflympics in 1939?

(a) United States   (b) Italy   (c) Sweden   (d) Austria

3. What is the role of Physiotherapist?

(a) To manage special needs children with movement disorder   (b) Help special needs children to develop find and gross motor skills

(c) To build communication of children with special needs.   (d) To work for the overall development of children with special needs

4. Paralympics is derived from .... word which means 'parallel to olympics'.

(a) Greek   (b) Latin   (c) Sanskrit   (d) Roman

5. Choose the incorrect statement.

(a) Special Olympics Bharat was initially named as Special Olympics India.

(b) Varied instruments and strategies are used in adaptive physical education.

(c) The first Summer Deaflympics was held in 1928 in Paris.

(d) Skiing, Snow-board, ice hockey are some of the games played in Winter Deaflympics.

6. The physical education instructor in a primary school wanted to include all the children of his class for a sports competition. Some students of his class were children with special needs.

Which type of sports should be designed for such students?

(a) Zonal competition   (b) Deaflympics

(c) Adaptive Sports   (d) Paralympics

Short Answer (SA) Type Questions

7. How are adaptive sports different from normal sports?

8. Explain the role of special educator in working with children with disabilities.

9. Write a short note on the formation of any one adaptive sports in India.

10. How adaptive physical education motivates children with disabilities?

11. What are adaptive sports? Which organisations promote adaptive sports?

Long Answer (LA) Type Questions

12. Write a detailed note on how Deaflympics came into existence.

13. Elucidate the role of occupational therapist for students with special needs.

Answers

1. (a)   *2.* (c)   *3.* (a)   *4.* (c)   *5.* (b)   *6.* (b)

Yoga

In this Chapter...

The practice of yoga is believed to have started with the very start of the Indian Civilisation. Many ancient sculptors, scriptures, seals and fossil remains of the Indus Valley Civilisation suggest that yoga was a part of the ancient Indian culture. Yoga has also been mentioned in *Mahabharata*, *Ramayana* and the *Upanishads* along with many other Indian scriptures.

Though Yoga was practiced in the ancient period, it was the great Sage Patanjali, who compiled *Yoga Sutras* in 147 BC, which presented its existing knowledge in a very systematic manner. Since then, Yoga has played a significant role in maintaining the mental and physical well-being of people all across the world.

Meaning of Yoga

The word 'Yoga' is derived from the Sanskrit word *'yuj'*, which means 'to join' or 'to unite'. This means that Yoga unites the individual's soul with the divine soul (*i.e.* God), a unification of *Atma* with *Parmatma*.

It implies the unification of the physical, mental, intellectual and spiritual aspects of a human being. It is also considered as a science which develops a person's consciousness.

The following definitions can be helpful to understand the meaning of Yoga

- According to **Maharishi Ved Vyas**, "Yoga is attaining the pose."
- According to **Patanjali**, "Suppression of modifications of the mind is Yoga."

- According to **Agam**, "The knowledge of Shiva and Shakti is Yoga."
- According to **Bhagwad Gita**, "Yoga is skill in action."

Importance of Yoga

The modern age is the age of stress, tension and anxiety. The improper lifestyle and the lack of proper relaxation make people physically tired and mentally tense.

Their lives are full of problems. They are always in a hurry and have no time for leisure. As a result, most of them be it rich or poor, do not live a peaceful, healthy or a happy life.

At such a juncture, yoga becomes very significant. The practice of yoga is not merely an exercise for the body. In fact, it is the knowledge that our ancestors developed to live a healthier, happier, peaceful and meaningful life. Thus, yoga is important in many ways, which are described as follows

1. **Brings about Physical Purity** Internal organs of our body can be cleansed by doing various yogic exercises.

   According to Ayurveda, our body is made of *Vaat* (airy elements), *Pitt* (fiery elements) and *Kaph* (watery elements). These elements must remain balanced for us to remain healthy.

   Yogic exercises which keep our bodies healthy and clean include *Basti, Dhoti, Kapalbhati, Nauli, Tratak* etc. For proper cleanliness and purity of our internal organs, we should perform these yogic exercises regularly.

2. **Prevents and Cures Diseases** There are various diseases which usually hamper the smooth functioning of our body. Yoga protects us from these diseases and also cures them. Various yogic exercises increase the body's immunity.

Diseases which can be cured by some *asanas*, if performed regularly, are given in the table below

Disease which can be Cured	Asanas to be Performed Regularly
Poor functioning of thyroid gland	*Halasana* / Plough pose and *Matsyasana* / Fish pose
PCOS in women (excess male hormone production)	*Dhanurasana* / Bow pose and *Bhujangasana* / Cobra pose
Arthritis	*Shishuasana* / *Child pose* and *Adho Mukha Svanasana* / Downward facing dog pose
Lower back pain	*Supta Matsyendrasana* / Supine Spinal Twist and *Marjaryasana*/Cat or Cow pose
Diabetes	*Ardha Matsyendrasana* / Half Spinal Twist and *Chakrasana* / Wheel pose
Indigestion / stomach disorder	*Apanasana* / Knees to chest pose and *Paschimottanasana* / Seated forward bend pose
Migraine (recurrent headache)	*Padmasana* / Lotus pose and *Padangusthasana*/Big Toe Pose
Liver problems	*Ardha Bhekasana* / Half Frog pose and *Parighasana* / Gate Pose
Depression	*Baddha Konasana* / Bound Angle pose and *Sukhasana* / Easy pose
Kidney disorders	*Salamba Bhujangasana* / Sphinx pose and *Naukasana* / Boat pose

3. **Improves Health in General** Yoga maintains and improves our health by making our respiratory, circulatory, nervous, digestive and excretory systems more efficient as well as strengthening our muscles.

4. **Reduces Mental Tension** In the modern world, most people are under constant stress and tension. Without peace of mind, people feel upset and disturbed. Yoga helps to reduce any stress and tension.

The *Pratyahara, Dharana* and *Dhyana* elements of Yoga help in bringing peace of mind. Some *asanas* like *Makarasana, Shavasana, Shalabhasana* and *Bhujangasana* benefit us by reducing stress and tension.

5. **Reduces Obesity and Beautifies the Body** Everyone wants to have a beautiful body. Obesity is a universal problem today and makes people prone to many diseases like high blood pressure, diabetes, heart diseases, stroke, gall bladder stones, cancer, gout, breathing problems etc.

Pranayam and yogic *asanas* like *Mayurasana* reduce obesity and make the body more beautiful.

6. **Gives Relaxation** When we indulge in any work, after some time we feel tired. At such times, we are unable to work further as we need relaxation.

Asanas like *Padmasana, Shavasana* and *Makarasana* as well as *Pranayama* helps in relaxing the body and mind, thus removing fatigue.

7. **Helps Maintain the Correct Posture** Due to the modern lifestyle of city dwellers, where most jobs are performed while being seated, deformities in posture are becoming common.

Practising *asanas* like *Sarvangasana, Mayurasana, Chakrasana, Bhujangasana, Vajrasana* and *Dhanurasana* helps to cure postural deformities and makes the practitioners of these *asanas* maintain correct posture.

8. **Increases Flexibility** Flexibility helps in moving the body efficiently. *Chakrasana, Dhanurasana, Shalabhasana, Halasana* and *Bhujangasana* helps in improving flexibility and prevents sports related injuries.

9. **Develops People Spiritually** *Padmasana* and *Siddhasana* improve the power of meditation and give better control over the mind to develop people spiritually. *Pranayama* also helps in spiritual development that brings peace in life.

10. **Improves Moral and Ethical Values** Nowadays, there is a declining trend in moral and ethical values. Following the first two elements of Yoga, *i.e. Yama* (meaning universal moral guidelines) and *Niyama* (meaning self-purification by discipline) helps in the development of moral and ethical values.

Elements of Yoga

In his description of the ancient Indian classical Yoga, Patanjali had classified Yoga into eight elements or *Ashtanga* (eight limbs).

These elements are also called the eight-fold paths or steps. These steps form a sequence from outer to inner self.

 17

Through this sequence, the ultimate goal of yoga, *i.e.* union of our soul with the divine can be achieved. These elements are as follows

1. **Yama** Yama contains the ethical rules of Hinduism. With the practice of Yama, one learns to self-restraint from struggle for survival. Yama contains 5 moral vows or codes of conduct, which are as follows

   - **Ahimsa** (Non-violence) It means that we must stay away from negative emotions like jealousy, hate anger, etc. and not harm any other living being.
   - **Satya** (Truthfulness) It means that we must be truth-ful in our thoughts, words and deeds at any cost.
   - **Asteya** (Non-stealing) It means that we must not use or even think of using others' objects, money or thoughts for our own benefit. We must be satisfied with what we have.
   - **Brahmacharya** (Celibacy) It means that we must stay away from anything that stimulates sexual desires. We must also not indulge in any sexual relations.
   - **Aparigraha** (Non-possessiveness) It means that we must live our life with minimum requirements. We must not desire to own any material possessions.

2. **Niyama** *Niyamas* are ethical practices that are related to the individual's body and senses. It contains essential teachings for self-maintenance including *Saucha, Santosh, Tapa, Swadhyaya* and *Isvara Pranidhana*, which are as follows

   - **Saucha** (Maintaining Cleanliness/Purity) It means that we must keep our mind, body and speech clean and pure.
     In yoga, special emphasis is given to cleanliness of internal organs using six *Shudhikriyas* or *Shatkarmas* such as *Neti kriya, Dhauti kriya* etc.
   - **Santosh** (Contentment) It means that we must develop a feeling of satisfaction in all situations of life.
   - **Tapa** (Discipline) It means that we must bear the difficulties, obstacles and complex situations in our life, in order to achieve the goal. We should also have the same spirit for all conflicts in our life like pleasure and pain, loss and gain.
   - **Swadhyaya** (Introspection or Study of the Self) It means the study of the various scriptures such as Vedas, Granths, Upanishads, etc. with devotion as well as the study of self.
   - **Ishvara Pranidhana** (Prayer or Surrendering to God) It means that as a devotee, a person must dedicate all

the deeds to God. He/she must think that all the facilities and prosperity such as body, mind, intelligence, etc. available to him are due to God. There must not exist any pride, ego and other impurities within him/her.

3. **Asanas** *Asanas* are a set of physical postures that improve strength and balance. These *asanas* are beneficial for the inner organs.

   There are various types of *asanas* such as corrective *asanas*, relaxative *asanas* and meditative *asanas*. These types of *asanas* have different types of effects on our body.

4. **Pranayama** It involves controlled breathing and is also practised with some *asanas*. It consists of three simple exercises, *i.e. Puraka* (Inhale), *Kumbhaka* (Retain the breath) and *Rechaka* (Exhale).

   It is considered beneficial for lungs and helps in boosting the count of red blood corpuscles. It improves heart and lung functioning and increases longevity.

   Ujjayi, Digra, Bahya, Aulom-Vilom Sheetali, Bhastrika, Nadi Sodhana, Kapalabhati etc are various types of *Pranayama*.

5. **Pratyahara** Pratyahara means to control our mind and senses. It is a self-control process where people become able to control their various senses.

   In other words, an individual stops responding to the external sensory world such as touch, taste, smell, etc. that hinders mental concentration and self-welfare. As a result, one starts meditating into the inner self.

6. **Dharana** It is the concentration of the mind and the first stage of meditation. You focus all your energy at one point without letting your mind get distracted, and discard all your random thoughts. The mind is fixed on one subject, topic or place.

7. **Dhyana** It is a process of complete constancy of mind. *Dharana* sets the stage for *dhyana*. When one starts focussing on a topic, the mind starts actively engaging with its focus.

   Thus, *dhyana* is the active modification of knowledge in complete stability and calmness.

8. **Samadhi** It is the ultimate union of an individual's soul with God. It is the stage where a person lose himself to God. The concepts of 'I', 'me' and 'mine' hold no significance for that person and he forgets himself completely.

Introduction to Asanas, Pranayama, Meditation and Yogic Kriyas

Asanas

According to **Patanjali,** *asana* means, *'sthiram sukham aasanam' i.e.* that position which is comfortable and steady.

In other words, Asana is a state of body in which it may be kept easily for an extended period in such a manner that all the organs and glands work most efficiently. Hence, Asanas are the means through which one can improve the health of mind and body.

Asanas also enhance the beauty of the body by reducing inappropriate accumulation of fat in the body. They help to regulate blood and oxygen flow. They bring flexibility and agility by stretching of muscles. They have no age restrictions and even old people can perform *asanas*.

Asanas are performed to improve flexibility, strength, and balance. The poses are not meant to simply be physical exercises but rather used as a mind-body practice to improve physical, mental, and spiritual health.

Types of Asanas

Asanas can be classified into three categories on the basis of its function. These are as follows

Types of Asana	Function	Examples
Meditative	Power of meditation is improved	*Padmasana, Siddhasana, Gaumukhasana, Swastikasana, Samasana, Veerasana* etc.
Reparative/ Relaxative	Removes fatigue and relaxes a person mentally and physically	*Shashankasana, Shavasana, Makarasana* etc.
Cultural / Corrective	Regulate and systematise bodily activities and provide energy	*Sheersasana, Sarvangasana, Matasyasana, Halasana, Bhujangasana, Shalabhasana, Dhanurasana, Vajrasana, Chakrasana* etc.

Pranayama

The word *'Paranayama'* is composed of two words, *prana* (meaning 'life') and *ayam* (meaning 'control'). Thus, it means 'control and regulation of the vital life force *i.e.* 'breathing.'

Pranayama strengthens the respiratory system, purifies the blood, soothes the nervous system, improves digestion, develops endurance and tones up the whole body.

It consists of three parts

1. **Puraka** (Inhale) When we breathe in, the chest expands, the diaphragm contracts and the ribs move outwards and up.

2. **Kumbhaka** (Retain) It consists of two parts, retaining the breath after complete inhalation (called 'internal *Kumbhaka* ') and retaining the breath after complete exhalation (called 'external *Kumbhaka* ').

3. **Rechaka** (Exhale) When we breathe out, the chest contracts, the diaphragm relaxes and the ribs move inwards and down.

Types of Pranayama

There are essentially various types or methods of *pranayama*. Some of them are

- *Suryabhedi pranayama* or right nostril breathing,
- *Ujjayi pranayama* or victorious breath,
- *Sheetkari pranayama* or the hissing breath,
- *Sheetali pranayama* or cooling breath,
- *Bhastrika pranayama* or bellows breath,
- *Bhramari pranayama* or bee breathing technique,
- *Plavini pranayama* or the floating breath,
- *Morcha pranayama* or swooning breath, etc.

Meditation

It is derived from the Sanskrit word *'Dhyana'*. It is the process of complete constancy or stability of mind.

According to **Patanjali,** *Dhyana* is "the concentration of *chitta* (the mind) on a *vritti* (an impulse) without any divergence".

It is described by Patanjali as *"tatra pratyaya ekatanata dhyanam"*, meaning a continuous and uninterrupted flow of attention towards the object of meditation.

As the 7th limb of yoga, it precedes the last step towards the achievement of goal of yoga. It essentially means to think, imagine, contemplate, and recollect. When such a perception starts, we call it *Dhyanavastha*.

When a person is in *Dhyanavastha*, he/she is only aware of his/her self and the object of meditation.

When perception starts directly without seeing any object, he/she gets the stage of *Dhyanavastha*, which is the prior stage of *samadhi*.

As a result, one modifies his/her knowledge and moves towards *samadhi*.

Benefits of Meditation

The various benefits of meditation are as follows

- It removes the agitation of the mind and creates calmness and peace inside.
- Practice of *dhyana* improves memory and attention in our day to day activities.
- *Dhyana* brings forth our hidden creativity.
- Regular practice of meditation can give good physical health and a sense of well-being.
- Negative emotions like anger can be slowly brought under our control with *dhyana*.
- The peace that one feels during meditation, radiates to others in our daily activities and creates a harmonious society, free of negative thoughts and feelings.

Yogic Kriyas

The human body requires both internal and external cleanliness for proper functioning. Generally, we carry out outer cleanliness, which is very easy, but inner cleanliness is slightly difficult.

Inner cleanliness of our body can be accomplished by practising six yogic *Kriyas*, also called *Shatkarmas* or *Shudhhi Kriyas*. These are as follows

1. **Neti** Nasal cleansing.
2. **Dhauti** Cleaning of digestive tract, especially oesophagus and stomach.
3. **Nauli** Abdominal massage.
4. **Kapalabhati** Purification of lungs and frontal lobe of brain.
5. **Basti** Colon cleaning.
6. **Trataka** Purification of the eye to overcome eye problems.

Benefits of Yogic Kriyas

The general benefits of performing these *kriyas* are as follows

- They help in overcoming many diseases completely, so they are effective in Yoga therapy.
- The practice of the *shatkarmas* creates harmony between body and mind.
- The different systems of the body are purified by the practice of the *shatkarmas*, so energy can flow through the body freely.
- Practising the *shatkarmas* increases the capacity to work, think, digest, taste, feel, experience etc.

Yoga for Concentration and Related Asanas

Concentration is one's power of focusing or attention on something. It is one of those essential attributes or skills that all individuals need to perform well in everything they do.

However, with stress and anxiety, people are often unable to concentrate on the task at hand.

Yoga, by its very nature, is said to be a great means to improve concentration and enable people to focus on their work effectively.

Patanjali mentioned about Yoga as, *"Yoga chitta vritti nirodha"* which means that yoga reduces the fluctuation of mind. Meditative exercises, various asanas helps to train mind and bring it to a relaxed state.

Various medical studies also show that yoga not only improves concentration, but also contributes to good mental energy and brings a balance to the body and the mind.

Some asanas which help to improve concentration include

Sukhasana (Easy Pose)

Sukhasana is a combination of two words *i.e.* 'sukh' meaning happiness or pleasure and 'asana' meaning posture. It is the foundation posture for seated meditation.

Procedure

- Sit on the floor with your legs straight in front of the body.
- Now, cross your legs such that each foot is under the opposite thighs, *i.e.* the left foot should be under right thigh and the right foot must be under left thigh.
- Keep your hands on your legs such that your palms are placed on your knees.
- Keep your head, neck and spine straight.
- Keep your legs and shoulder relaxed.
- Close your eyes and practice deep breathing.

Benefits

- It strengthens muscles of the back and improves body posture.
- It has relaxing effects on mind and body.
- It builds physical and mental balance as well as concentration.
- It is helpful in reducing stress and anxiety.
- It creates flexibility in ankle, knee and hip joints.
- It increases the functioning of the glands.
- It helps in curing arthritis and knock-knees.

Contraindication

The individuals who have knee injury or have severe knee pain or lower back pain should not perform this asana for longer duration.

Sukhasana

Tadasana (Mountain Pose)

Tadasana is made from two words *i.e.* 'tada' meaning mountain or palm tree and 'asana' meaning posture. It is the foundation of all of the standing yoga asanas.

Procedure

- Stand straight with your feet slightly apart and your hands by your side.
- Inhale deeply and slowly raise your arms upwards, then interlock your fingers.
- Raise your heels and stand on your toes.
- Feel your body stretching and look up.
- Place your body weight on your toes and stretch out your shoulders, arms, and chest up.
- Hold this pose for a few moments.
- Exhale and return to the starting position.

Benefits

- It improves posture.
- It strengthens and increases the flexibility of thighs, knees, and ankles.
- It firms abdomen and buttocks.
- It helps to cure the disease sciatica.
- It helps in increasing height.
- It improves the function of respiratory and digestive organs.
- It strengthen the nervous system.
- It is good to improve balance and concentration as well as increase alertness.

- It relieves tension, aches, and pains throughout the body.

Tadasana

Contraindications

- Don't do this pose, if you suffer from insomnia/sleeplessness.
- If you experience a headache, stop immediately.
- If you take any blood thinning medications or have low blood pressure, avoid doing this pose without consulting a doctor.

Padmasana (Lotus Pose)

Padmasana is made of two words *i.e.* 'padma' meaning lotus and 'asana' meaning posture. This yogic exercise primarily means setting and meditating in a position without any movement.

Procedure

- Sit on the floor or on a mat with legs stretched out in front of you, while keeping the spine erect.
- Bend the right knee and place it on the left thigh. Make sure that the sole of the feet point upward and the heel is close to the abdomen.
- Now, repeat the same step with the other leg (*i.e.* left knee on right thigh).
- Place your hands on the knees in mudra position.
- Keep the head straight and spine erect.
- Hold and continue with gentle long breaths in and out.

Benefits

- It calms the brain and increases the focus of mind.
- It increases concentration.
- It stimulates the pelvis, spine, abdomen, and bladder.

- It stretches the ankles and knees.
- It helps in reducing blood pressure and muscular tension.
- It helps in reducing abdominal fat.
- It strengthens the hip and knee joints.

Contraindications

- Do not perform this asana if you are suffering from ankle injury or knee injury.
- It is considered to be an intermediate to advanced pose. Thus, do not perform this pose without sufficient prior experience or unless you have the supervision of an experienced teacher.

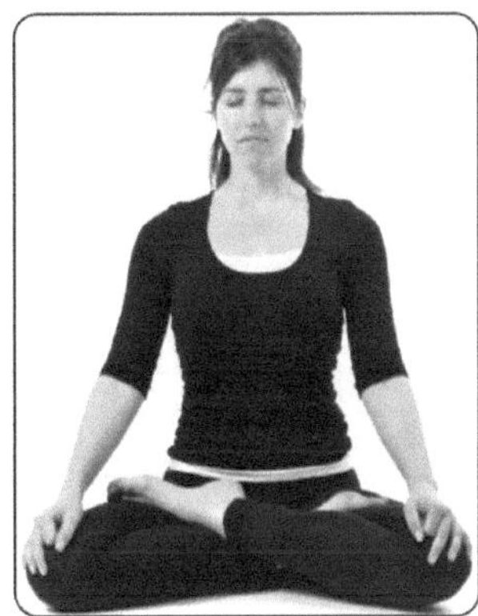

Padmasana

Shashankasana (Rabbit/Hare Pose)

Shashankasana has been derived from two Sanskrit words *i.e.* 'shashanka' which means rabbit or hare and 'asana' means posture.

Also known as the 'Crescent Moon Posture' (shashanka also means moon), the final pose of this asana resembles a leaping rabbit.

Procedure

- Sit in a kneeling position with your knees fully bent and hands on the thighs (Vajrasana).
- Straighten the back.
- Inhale and slowly raise the arms, above the head. The arms should be in line with the shoulders.
- Now, exhale and bend forward.
- The arms, trunk and head should remain in one line.
- The forehead and arms should rest on the floor in front of the knees.
- Relax the whole body and let the elbows also rest on the floor.

- Inhale and exhale slowly.
- Inhale and raise your arms and trunk to the vertical position.

Shashankasana

Benefits

- It is known for abdomen toning.
- It helps in stretching and strengthening of the arms, shoulders and upper back.
- It helps in ankle and knee strengthening and flexibility.
- It helps in posture correction through treatment of the 'dropping shoulders' symptom.
- It relieves fatigue and promotes concentration.
- It helps in relieving stress, anxiety and calms the mind.
- It improves the blood supply in the head and therefore, nourishes the brain and the eyes.
- It stimulates the functioning of the glands.
- It controls diabetes.

Contraindictation

Do not perform this asana if you are suffering from backache or slipped disc, knee pain, migraine, abdominal injury or high blood pressure.

Naukasana (Boat Pose)

Naukasana is comprised of two words *i.e.* 'nauka' means boat and 'asana' means posture. This yoga posture has been named based on the shape it takes *i.e.* of a boat.

Procedure

- Lie on your back with your feet together and arms beside your body.
- Take a deep breath in and as you exhale, lift your chest and feet off the ground, stretching your arms towards your feet.
- Your eyes, fingers and toes should be in a line.
- Feel the tension in your navel area as the abdominal muscles contract.

- Keep breathing deeply and easily while maintaining the pose.
- As you exhale, come back to the ground slowly and relax.

Benefits

- It strengthens the back and abdominal muscles.
- It tones the leg and arm muscles.
- It is useful for people with hernia.
- It helps to remove belly fat.
- It improves digestion.
- It improves the circulation of blood.
- It gives strength to thigh, hips, shoulder and neck.
- It helps in regulating the sugar level in the blood.

Contraindications

- Do not practice this yoga pose if you have low blood pressure, severe headache, migraine, or if you have suffered from some chronic diseases or spinal disorders in the recent past.
- Asthma and heart patients are advised to avoid this pose.
- Women should avoid doing this pose during pregnancy and during the first two days of the menstrual cycle.

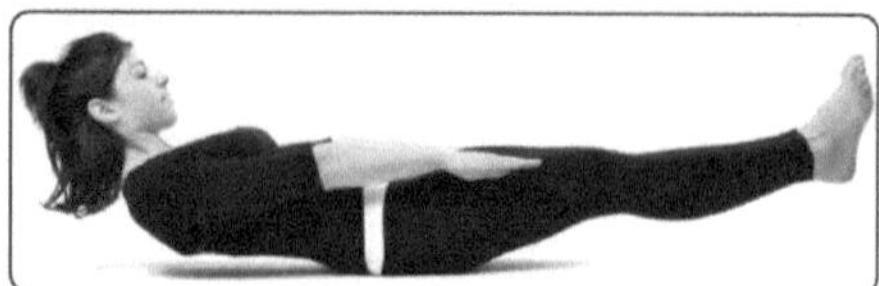

Naukasana

Vrikshasana (Tree Pose)

The name of this asana comes from the two Sanskrit words *i.e.* 'vriksa or vriksha' meaning tree, and 'asana' meaning posture. This posture is a close replica of the steady, yet graceful stance of a tree.

Procedure

- Stand tall and straight with arms by the side of your body.
- Bend your right knee and place the right foot up on your left thigh. The sole of the foot should be placed flat and firmly near the root of the thigh.
- Make sure that your left leg is straight.
- Once you are well balanced, take a deep breath in, gracefully raise your arms over your head from the side, and bring your palms together in *'Namaste' mudra* (hands-folded position).
- Look straight ahead in front of you.

- Ensure that your spine is straight.
- Keep taking in long deep breaths. With each exhalation, relax the body more and more. Just be with the body and the breath with a gentle smile on your face.
- With slow exhalation, gently bring down your hands from the sides. You may gently release the right leg.
- Now, stand tall and straight as you did at the beginning of the posture. Repeat this pose with the left leg off the ground on the right thigh.

Vrikshasana

Benefits

- This pose leaves you in a state of rejuvenation and relaxation.
- It brings balance and equilibrium to your mind.
- It helps improve concentration.
- This posture has been found to relieve some cases of sciatica.
- It strengthens the spine while improving both balance and poise.
- It tones the leg muscles while making the ligaments and tendons of the feet stronger.
- The knees become stronger, and the hip joints are loosened.
- The eyes, inner ears, and shoulders are also strengthened in this pose.
- It makes you stable, flexible, and patient.
- It enhances concentration and activates all the mental faculties.

Contraindication

Avoid doing this posture, if you are suffering from migraine, insomnia, low or high blood pressure, knee problems and hip injury.

Garudasana (Eagle Pose)

The name comes from the Sanskrit words *i.e.* 'garuda' meaning eagle, and 'asana' meaning posture. It is a standing balancing asana in modern yoga as exercise.

Procedure

- Take a standing position.
- Bend your right leg and twist it around the left one.
- Ensure that right thigh should be in front of the left thigh. The top of the right foot should place on the calf of the left leg.
- Now, bend your elbows and place them on the front of the chest.
- Twist your forearms around each other, the left elbow should remain below.
- Bring your palms together to resemble an eagle's beak.
- Now, bend the left knee and lower the body in slow motion, until the tip of the right big toe touches the floor.
- Hold this position for around 20 to 30 seconds with steady breathing.
- Now, release the posture and return to standing position.
- After completing this procedure, repeat this on the other side.

Benefits

- It stretches the hips, thighs, shoulders and upper back.
- It improves balance.
- It strengthens the calves and ankles.
- It helps alleviate sciatica and rheumatism.
- It loosens the muscles of legs and hips, making them more flexible.

Contraindication

Avoid practicing this pose if you've had a recent knee, ankle or elbow injury.

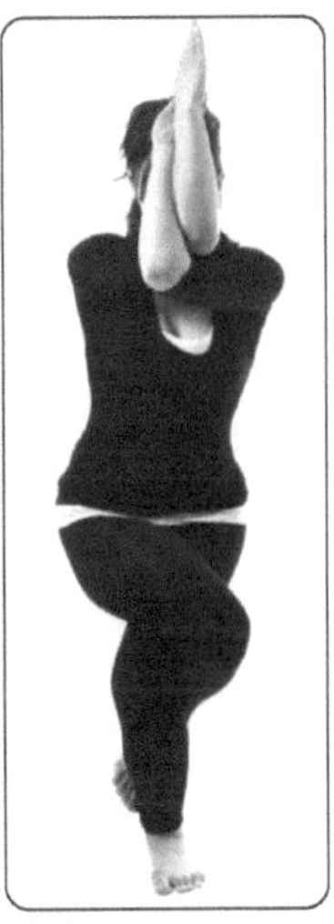

Garudasana

Chapter Practice

Objective Questions

• Multiple Choice Questions

1. Yoga has been mentioned in _________.
(a) Mahabharata   (b) Ramayana
(c) Upanishads   (d) All of these
Ans. (d) Yoga has been mentioned in Mahabharata, Ramayana and Upanishads. It is an integral part of Indian culture.

2. From where do we derive the elements of yoga?
(a) Bhagwad Gita
(b) Yoga-sutra
(c) Upanishads
(d) Ramayana
Ans. (b) The elements of yoga are derived from Yoga-sutras, which were compiled by Patanjali in 147 BC.

3. Match the following.

List I	List II
A. Vaat	1. Fiery element
B. Pitt	2. Yogic element
C. Kaph	3. Airy element
D. Tratak	4. Watery element

Codes

	A	B	C	D			A	B	C	D
(a)	4	3	1	2		(b)	2	1	4	3
(c)	1	3	2	4		(d)	3	1	4	2

Ans. (d) The correct match is A-3, B-1, C-4 and D-2.

4. The yogic elements that includes the study of self is _________.
(a) Pratyahara   (b) Dhyana
(c) Swadhyaya   (d) Rechaka
Ans. (c) The yogic element that includes the study of self is called swadhyaya. Swadhyaya means interospection or study of the self. etc.

5. Match the following.

List I	List II
A. Santosh	1. Non-possessiveness
B. Brahmacharya	2. Purity
C. Saucha	3. Contentment
D. Aparigraha	4. Celibacy

Codes

	A	B	C	D			A	B	C	D
(a)	3	4	2	1		(b)	1	2	3	4
(c)	2	3	1	4		(d)	4	1	3	2

Ans. (a) The correct match is A-3, B-4, C-2 and D-1.

6. Swami ji described about one of the elements of yoga. He said that it is the concentration of mind and the first stage of meditation. All energies are focussed at one point and the mind is not distracted. Swami ji is talking about which stage?
(a) Dharana   (b) Dhyana
(c) Pratyahara   (d) Pranayama
Ans. (a) Swami ji is talking about Dharana the first stage of meditation. The mind is prepared to be fixed at one subject, topic or place.

7. Sukhasana strengthens muscles of the back and improves _________.
(a) body posture   (b) spine
(c) focus of mind   (d) abdomen
Ans. (a) Sukhasana strengthens muscles of the back and improves body posture.

8. Human body requires both internal and external cleanliness for proper functioning. Outer cleanliness is easy but inner cleanliness is slightly difficult. The inner cleanliness of the body can be attained by practicing which of the following kriyas?
(a) Neti   (b) Basti
(c) Nauli   (d) All of these
Ans. (d) The inner cleanliness of the body can be attained by Neti, Basti, Nauli. Dhamti, Kapalabhati and Trataka are also ways of inner cleanliness.

9. Identify the asana shown in the image.

(a) Tadasana
(b) Sukhasana
(c) Shashankasana
(d) Naukasana

Ans. (b) The asana shown in the image is Sukhasana. It is done in sitting position and is the foundation posture for seated meditation.

10. Ishani is a yoga teacher. His students are middle aged people facing stiffness of muscles of shoulders and upper back. He gave them a demonstration on how to do an asana. See the image below and identify the asana shown by Ishani.

(a) Mayurasana   (b) Sulabhasana
(c) Shashankasana   (d) Vrikshasana

Ans. (c) The asana shown by Ishan is Shashankasana. It is also called rabbit or hare pose. It is beneficial for reducing the stiffness of muscles.

11. When we indulge in any kind of mental work, after sometime we feel tired. Our mind can no longer focus. At such times, we are unable to work further as we need relaxation.

Which among the following is an asana that relaxes the body and mind thus removing fatigue?
(a) Padmasana
(b) Sukhasana
(c) Shashankasana
(d) All of the above

Ans. (d) All of the asanas i.e. Padmasana, Sukhasana and Shashankasana are the asanas that relaxes the mind. Thus, remove fatigue.

12. Which of the following is the correct contraindication of the asana shown below.

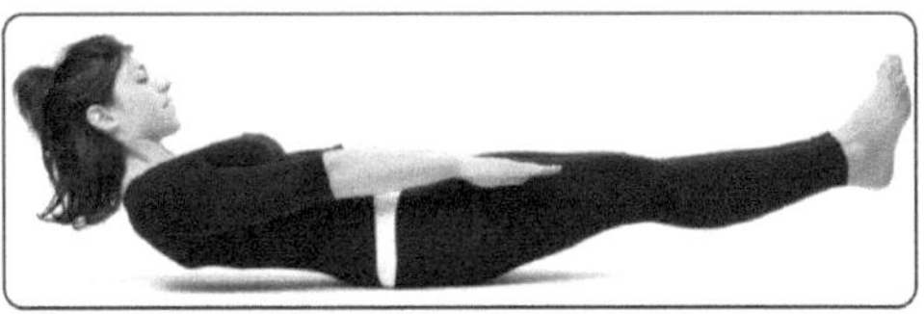

(a) Avoid doing if you suffers from insomnia
(b) Avoid doing if you have high blood pressure
(c) Avoid doing if you have ankle or elbow injury
(d) Avoid doing if you have Asthama or are a heart patient

Ans. (d) The asana in the given image is Naukasana. Avoid doing if you have Asthama or are a heart patient, is the correct contraindication of this asana.

13. The english name for 'Garudasana' is ________.
(a) Bird pose
(b) King pose
(c) Eagle pose
(d) Moon pose

Ans. (c) The English name for 'Garudasana' is Eagle pose as the posture made in this asana resembles the eagle.

14. Which of the following asanas does not help in improving concentration?
(a) Sukhasana   (b) Tadasana
(c) Chakrasana   (d) Padmasana

Ans. (a) Chakrasana does not help in improving concentration.

15. Match the following.

	List I		List II
A.	Sciatica	1.	Hare pose
B.	Arthiritis	2.	Mountain pose
C.	Diabetes	3.	Lotus pose
D.	Blood Pressure	4.	Easy pose

Codes

	A	B	C	D
(a)	3	1	4	2
(b)	1	2	3	4
(c)	2	4	1	3
(d)	4	3	2	1

Ans. (c) The correct match is A-2, B-4, C-1 and D-3.

● Assertion-Reasoning MCQs

Directions (Q. Nos. 1-4) *Each of these questions contains two statements, Assertion (A) and Reason (R). Each of these questions also has four alternative choices, any one of which is the correct answer. You have to select one of the codes (a), (b), (c) and (d) given below.*

Codes

(a) Both A and R are true and R is the correct explanation of A

(b) Both A and R are true, but R is not the correct explanation of A

(c) A is true, but R is false

(d) A is false, but R is true

1. Assertion (A) Yoga unites the individual's soul with the divine soul.

Reason (R) The word 'Yoga' is derived from the Sanskrit word Yuj which means to unite.

Ans. (b) The assertion is true as Samadhi is an element of yoga that unites the individual's soul with divine soul. The reason is also true as the meaning of yoga is to join and is derived from Sanskrit word Yuj. But reason do not explains assertion. Thus, both A and R are true, but R is not the correct explanation of A.

2. Assertion (A) Yoga is not effective for depression.

Reason (R) Yoga helps in maintaining correct posture.

Ans. (d) Assertion is false as depression is a psychological condition and yoga deals with physical, mental, intellectual aspects, so it can help in depression too. Reason is true as yogic asanas help in maintaining correct posture and improves strength and balance. Thus, A is false, but R is true.

3. Assertion (A) Pratyahara is the ultimate union of an individual's soul with God.

Reason (R) Pranayama involves controlled breathing.

Ans. (d) Assertion is false as Pratyahara means to control our mind and senses. Reason is true as Pranayama involves controlled breathing and is also practised with some asana. Thus, A is false, but R is true.

4. Assertion (A) Naukasana is good for reducing belly fat.

Reason (R) Tadasana is performed in a sitting position.

Ans. (c) Assertion is true as Naukasana is a good asana that improves digestion and help in removing belly fat. The reason is false as Tadasana is done in standing position. Thus, A is true, but R is false.

● Case Based MCQs

1. The Yoga instructor advised 62 years old Mr. Verma to do Yoga daily. He showed him the asana called Eagle pose as it will help to make muscles of legs flexible.

Based on this case, answer the following questions

(i) Eagle pose is used to treat ______ and ______.

(a) sciatica and rheumatism　(b) hairfall and back pain

(c) eyes and shoulders　　　(d) knee pain and abdomen

Ans. (a) Eagle pose is used to treat sciatica and rheumatism.

(ii) Eagle pose asana is done in which pose?

(a) Standing　　　　(b) Sitting

(c) Lying　　　　　(d) All of these

Ans. (a) Eagle pose asana is done in standing position. Here the hands and legs are crossed out in the front position.

(iii) Which of the following is the contraindication of Eagle pose?

(a) Avoid if had a knee injury

(b) Avoid if had an ankle injury

(c) Both (a) and (b)

(d) None of the above

Ans. (c) The contraindication of Eagle pose is that it should be avoided if there is a knee or ankle injury.

2. Mahesh is a yoga instructor in a school. He explained about the 8 concepts or elements of yoga to his students.

8 elements of Yoga are the eight fold paths or steps to reach the ultimate goal of Yoga.

(i) Which of the elements of Yoga focus on controlled breathing techniques?

(a) Niyama　　　　(b) Pratyahara

(c) Dharana　　　　(d) Pranayama

Ans. (d) Pranayama is a systematic and rhythmic control of breathing techniques.

(ii) Which Yoga element contains 5 moral vows or codes of conduct?

(a) Yama　　　　(b) Niyama

(c) Dhyana　　　(d) Asana

Ans. (a) Yama contains five moral vows which are ahimsa, satya, asteya, brahmacharya and Aparigraha.

(iii) The concepts of I, me, mine hold no significance in which element?

(a) Dharana　　　　(b) Pratyahara

(c) Samadhi　　　　(d) Dhyana

Ans. (c) In samadhi, which is the eighth and last element of Yoga, the concepts of I, me and mine hold no significance.

PART 2
Subjective Questions

• Short Answer (SA) Type Questions

1. Enlist nine reasons, why the practice of Yoga is important for us.

Ans. Nine reasons why the practice of Yoga is important for us are as follows
- It brings about physical purity.
- It prevents and cures diseases by providing immunity to the body.
- It reduces mental tension.
- It reduces obesity and beautifies the body.
- It relaxes the body and mind.
- It corrects and maintains posture.
- It increases flexibility.
- It develops people spiritually.
- It improves moral and ethical values.

2. What is the meaning of the second element of Yoga? What are its five parts?

Ans. The second element of Yoga is called Niyama, which contains five esssential teachings for self-maintenance. These teachings are as follows
- **Shaucha** It means maintaining cleanliness of the body, both internal and external.
- **Santosh** (Contentment) It means to develop a feeling of satisfaction in what we have.
- **Tapas** (Discipline) It means to bear the complex situations of our life to achieve the goal.
- **Swadhyaya** It means the study of various scriptures for introspection.
- **Isvaraparanidhana** It means prayer or surrendering to God.

3. What do you mean by Yama? What are the five basic vows mentioned in it?

Ans. Yama is the first element of Yoga, which teaches that we should not corrupt our souls by indulging in wrongful activities. It contains five basic vows which everyone should have. These are as follows
- **Ashimsa** (Non-violence) It means not harming any other living being.
- **Satya** (Truthfulness) It means that we must be truthful in our thoughts, words and deeds.
- **Asteya** (Non-stealing) It means that we should not steal and remain satisfied with what we have.
- **Brahmacharya** (Celibacy) It means that we must not indulge in any sexual desires.
- **Aparigraha** (Non-possessiveness) It means that we should not desire material possessions.

4. What are asanas and how are they beneficial?

Ans. Asanas are a set of a steady and comfortable postures perfomed in a way to make the activities of the organs and glands of the body more efficient, besides bringing many other benefits. Benefits of Asanas are as follows
- They benefit the internal organs by helping to regulate blood and oxygen flow.
- They bring flexibility and agility by stretching of muscles.
- They help to maintain correct posture.

5. Asanas can be classified into how many categories. Explain the categories briefly.

Ans. Asanas can be classified in three categories. These are as follows
  (i) **Meditative** This types of asanas improve the power of meditation. Examples are Padmasana (lotus pose), Siddhasana (accomplished pose) and Gaumukhasana (cow face pose).
  (ii) **Reparative or relaxing** This types of asanas removes fatigue and relaxes a person mentally and physically. Examples are Shashankasana (hare/ rabbit pose), Shavasana (corpse pose) and Makarasana (crocodile pose).
  (iii) **Cultural/Corrective** This types of asanas regulate and systematise the bodily activities and provide energy. Examples are Sheershasana (head stand), Bhujangasana (cobra pose) and Matasyasana (fish pose).

6. What do you understand by pranayama? Describe its three parts in detail.

Ans. The word pranayama is composed of two words, prana (meaning life) and ayam (meaning control). Thus, it means control and regulation of the vital life force or energy.

It consists of three parts, which are as follows
  (i) **Puraka** (Inhale) When we breathe in, the chest expands, the diaphragm contracts and the ribs move outwards and up.
  (ii) **Kumbhaka** (Retain) It consists of two parts, retaining the breath after complete inhalation called internal Kumbhaka and retaining the breath after complete exhalation called 'external Kumbhaka'.
  (iii) **Rechaka** (Exhale) When we breathe out, the chest contracts, the diaphragm relaxes and the ribs move inwards and down.

7. Write a short note on meditation.

Ans. Meditation is the process of complete constancy or stability of mind. It is described by Patanjali as 'tatra pratyaya ekatanata dhyanam' meaning a continuous and uninterrupted flow of attention towards the object of meditation.

It essentially means to think, imagine, contemplate and recollect everything about the object.

The various benefits of meditation are as follows

- It removes the agitation of the mind and creates calmness and peace inside.
- It improves memory and attention in our day to day activities.
- Dhyana brings forth our hidden creativity.
- The peace the one feels during meditation, radiates to others in our daily activities and creates a harmonious society, free of negative thoughts and feelings.
- Regular practice of meditation can give good physical health and a sense of well-being.

8. What are the six yogic kriyas and what are the functions of these kriyas?

Ans. The six yogic kriyas and the function of each of them are as follows

- (i) **Neti** It helps in nasal cleansing.
- (ii) **Dhauti** It helps in cleaning of oesophagus and stomach.
- (iii) **Nauli** It used in abdominal massage to improve functioning of the whole digestive system.
- (iv) **Kapalabhati** It helps in purification of lungs and frontal lobe of brain.
- (v) **Basti** It is a technique of replenishing the body internally by Cleansing the colon completely.
- (vi) **Trataka** It is used in purification of the eye to overcome eye problems.

9. Give the Sanskrit names and their equivalent English meanings of any four asanas in Yoga which help in improving concentration.

Write one benefit of performing each of these asanas.

Ans. The four asanas in Yoga which help in improving concentration and their additional benefits are as follows

- *Tadasana*, is called the palm tree pose or mountain pose. It helps to gain sense of balance, opens up the chest cavity for breathing exercises, stimulates the thyroid gland and helps increase height.
- *Sukhasana*, is called the easy pose. It calms the wind, strengthens the back and stretches the knees and ankles.
- *Padmasana*, is called the lotus pose. It calms the mind, increases awareness and attentiveness and restores energy levels.

- *Shashankasana*, is called the hare pose. It relaxes the body, relieves depression and gives the upper body a good stretch.

10. Explain the procedure for performing Sukhasana.

Ans. The procedure for performing Sukhasana is as follows

- Sit on the floor with your legs straight in front of the body.
- Now, cross your legs such that each foot is under the opposite thighs, i.e. the left foot should be under right thigh and the right foot must be under left thigh.
- Keep your hand on your legs such that your palms are placed on your kness.
- Keep your head, neck and spine straight.
- Keep your legs and shoulder relaxed.
- Close your eyes and practice deep breathing.

11. What is Tadasana? What are the benefits of Tadasana?

Ans. Tadasana is one of the yogic asana that is done in standing posture. It is also called as mountain pose or palm tree. It is the foundation of all standing yoga asanas.

Tadasana as a yogic exercises has many benefits. These are as follows

- It improves posture.
- It strengthens and increases the flexibility of thighs, knees and ankles.
- It firms abdomen and buttocks.
- It helps in inceasing height.
- It improves the function of respiratory and digestive organs.
- It strengthen the nervous system.
- It is good to improve balance and concentration as well as increase alertness.

12. What are the contraindications of Tadasana and Sukhasana?

Ans. The contraindications of Tadasana are as follows

- Don't do this pose, if you suffer from insomnia/sleeplessness.
- If you experience a headache, stop immediately.
- If you take any blood thinning medications or have low blood pressure, avoid doing this pose without consulting a doctor.

The Contraindications of Sukhasana are as follow

- The individuals who have knee injury or have severe knee pain or lower back pain should not perform this asana for longer duration.

13. What are the benefits of Padmasana?

Ans. Padmasana is also called Lotus pose. It is done in a sitting posture. The benefits of Padmasana are as follows

- It calms the brain and increases the focus of mind.
- It increases concentration.
- It stimulates the pelvis, spine, abdomen and bladder.

* It stretches the ankles and knees.
* It helps in reducing blood pressure and muscular tension.
* It helps in reducing abdominal fat.
* It strengthens the hip and knee joints.

14. Explain the procedure for performing Vrikshasana.

Ans. The procedure for performing Vrikshasana is as follows

* Stand tall and straight with arms by the side of your body.
* Bend your right knee and place the right foot high up on your left thigh.
* Make sure that your left leg is straight.
* Once you are well balanced, gracefully raise your arms over your head from the side, and bring your palms together in 'Namaste' mudra (hand-folded position).
* Look straight ahead in front of you.
* Ensure that your spine is straight.
* Now, stand tall and straight as you did at the beginning of the posture. Repeat this pose with the left leg off the ground on the right thigh.

15. Explain the procedure for performing Garudasana.

Ans. The procedure for performing Garudasana is as follows

* Take a standing position.
* Bend your right leg and twist it around the left one.
* Ensure that right thigh should be in front of the left thigh. The top of the right foot should place on the calf of the left leg.
* Now, bend your elbows and place them on the front of the chest.
* Twist your forearms around each other, the left elbow should remain below.
* Bring your palms together to resemble an eagle's beak.
* Now, bend the left knee and lower the body in slow motion, until the tip of the right big toe touches the floor.
* After completing this procedure, repeat this on the other side.

• Long Answer (LA) Type Questions

1. What is Yoga? Discuss any three elements of Yoga in Brief.

Ans. The word 'Yoga' is derived from the Sanskrit word Yuj, which means 'to join' or to unite. Thus, Yoga unites the individual's soul with the divine soul (i.e. God).

It also implies the unification of the physical, mental, intellectual and spiritual aspects of a human being. According to Patanjali, Yoga has eight elements known as Ashtanga.

Three elements of Yoga are discussed as follows

(i) **Yama** This contains five basic ethical rules that every person should possess. These five moral codes of conduct are Ahimsa (Non-violence), Satya (Truthfulness), Asteya (Non-stealing), Brahmacharya (Celibacy) and Aparigraha (Non-possessiveness).

(ii) **Niyama** It contains essential teachings for self-maintenance including Saucha (Maintaining cleanliness of the body/purity), Santosh (Contentment), Tapa (Discipline), Swadhyana (Introspection or studying the self) and Isvara Pranidhana (Prayer or surrendering to God.)

(iii) **Asanas** These are a set of physical postures that improve strength and balance. These asanas are beneficial for the inner organs, help to regulate blood and oxygen flow, bring flexibility and agility by stretching of muscles and help to maintain posture.

2. Explain the Pranayama, Pratyahara, Dharana, Dhyana and Samadhi element of Yoga.

Ans. **Pranayama** It consists of three simple exercises Puraka (Inhale), Kumbhaka (Retain) and Rechaka (Exhale). It involves controlled breathing, improves heart and lung functioning and increases longevity.

Pratyahara It means to control our mind and senses. In other words, an individual stops responding to the external sensory word such as touch, taste, smell, etc. that hinders mental concentration and self-welfare.

Dharana It is the first stage of meditation. You focus all your energy at one point without letting your mind get distracted. The mind, then get focused on one topic object or thing.

Dhyana Dharana sets the stage for dhyana. It is a process of complete constancy of mind. When one starts focusing on a topic, the mind starts actively engaging with its focus. Thus, dhyana is the active modification of knowledge in complete stability and calmness.

Samadhi It is the ultimate union of ones soul with God. It is the stage where one loses oneself to God. The concepts of I, me and mine hold no significance for that person.

3. Write the procedure of performing the Shashankasana, also called the hare pose.

Ans. The procedure of performing the Shashankasana is as follows

* Sit in the kneeling pose with knees fully bent. Place your hands on the thighs and breathe in a relaxed manner.
* Raise both your hands above the head, palms facing forward. The arms should be in line with the shoulders.
* Slowly bend down and bring the hands forward, till the hands and forehead touch the ground. Exhale while you are bending forward.
* In the final position, the forehead and hands rest on the ground. Rest in this position for as long as you are comfortable and breathe rhythmically.
* Exhale slowly and come back to the starting position (kneeling pose). Repeat this process 5 to 10 times depending on time and comfort.

4. Write the procedure for performing Naukasana and also write its benefits.

Ans. The procedure for performing Naukasana is as follows

- Lie on your back with your feet together and arms beside your body.
- Take a deep breath in and as you exhale, lift your chest and feet off the ground, stretching your arms towards your feet.
- Your eyes, fingers and toes should be in a line.
- Feel the tension in your navel area as the abdominal muscles contract.
- Keep breathing deeply and easily while maintaining the pose.
- As you exhale, come back to the ground slowly and relax.

Naukasana has various benefits, which are as follows

- It strengthens the back and abdominal muscles.
- It tones the leg and arm muscles.
- It is useful for people with hernia.
- It helps to remove belly fat.
- It improves digestion.
- It improves the circulation of blood.
- It gives strength to thigh, hips, shoulder and neck.
- It helps in regulating the sugar level in the blood.

• Case Based Questions

1. Shivam is a student of class XI and is facing problem of poor concentration. During a recent medical check-up of school he was advised to practice Yogasana (as given in syllabus) and participate in sports activities for curing it.

Based on this case answer the following questions.

(i) What are relaxative asanas?

Ans. Asanas that removes fatigue and relaxes a person mentally or physically are called relaxative asanas.

(ii) How Yoga helps in concentration?

Ans. Yoga improves power of focusing or attention. It trains the mind, reduces fluctuation of mind which helps in concentration.

2. The physical education teacher of ABC school made a chart for the students to explain about the 8 elements of yoga.

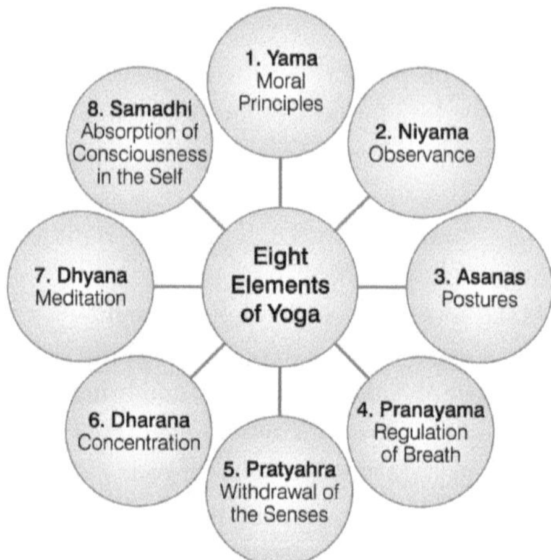

(i) Which moral vows are contained in Yama element?

Ans. The moral vows contained in Yama element are Ahimsa, Satya, Asteya, Brahmacharya and Aprigraha.

(ii) What does the word 'Yoga' imply?

Ans. The word 'Yoga' implies the unification of the physical, mental, intellectual and spiritual aspects of a human being.

3. Some students of class XI complained to their teacher that they are facing anxiety and stress due to the upcoming examinations.

Based on the case, answer the following questions.

(i) Which asana is suggested by the teacher to reduce anxiety and stress?

Ans. Sukhasana is suggested by the teacher to reduce anxiety and stress.

(ii) What are the benefits of the 'Lotus pose'?

Ans. The Padmasana or Lotus pose helps in meditation and concentration. It also calms the brain, increases awareness and attentiveness and restores energy levels.

Chapter Test

Multiple Choice Questions

1. Which is the seventh element of Yoga?

   (a) Dhyana   (b) Yama   (c) Pratyahara   (d) Samadhi

2. Cleaning of internal organs is a parts of ________ .

   (a) Dhauti kriya   (b) Swadhaya   (c) Tapa   (d) Apoigraha

3. According to whom the definition of Yoga is simply to attain the pose?

   (a) Patanjali   (b) Maharishi Ved Vyas   (c) Agam   (d) None of the above

4. Which is the foundation posture for seated meditation?

   (a) Padmasana   (b) Sukhasana   (c) Shashankasana   (d) Garudasana

5. Find the incorrect statement

   (a) Yama contains 5 moral vows or codes of conduct
   (b) Ishavara Pranidhana means study of scriptures
   (c) Niyama are ethical practices related to body and senses
   (d) Samadhi is ultimate union of a soul with God.

6. Pranayam means control and regulation of the vital life force i.e. breathing. Pranayam is the fourth element of yoga. It strengthens the respiratory system, soothes the nervous system and tones up the whole body. Pranayam is an important yogic kriya and is practised in India from ancient times. it consists of three parts. From the given options, find out the three parts of Pranayama.

   (a) Neti, Dhauti, Nauli   (b) Kapalbhati, Basti, Trataka
   (c) Puraka, Kumbhaka, Rechaka   (d) Dharana, Dhyana, Samadhi

Short Answer (SA) Type Questions

7. What is the other name of Tadasana? Explain its procedure.

8. Briefly explain the element of Dhayana and Samadhi.

9. What are the benefits of yogic kriyas?

10. What is Ishvara Paranidhara?

11. Explain the procedure of doing Naukasana.

Long Answer (SA) Type Questions

12. Yoga is known to prevent and cure various diseases. List in tabular form, five lifestyle diseases which can be cured by performing yogic asanas and two asanas which help in curing/preventing each of these diseases.

13. Explain the procedure and contraindications of Padmasana.

Answers

1. (a)   *2.* (a)   *3.* (b)   *4.* (b)   *5.* (b)   *6.* (c)

Physical Activity and Leadership Training

In this Chapter...

- Introduction to Leadership
- Qualities of a Leader
- Role of a Leader
- Adventure Sports
- Safety Measures to Prevent Sports Injuries

Physical education and its activities ensures the growth and development of many qualities including intelligence, firm determination, cooperation, etc. One of these qualities essential to the field is leadership.

Introduction to Leadership

Leadership is defined as "the activity of inspiring people to perform and engage in achieving a goal." It means to lead a group of people or an organisation in reaching a particular target.

Leadership is a unique skill that cannot be taught but can be learned through observing others. It means to have a clear vision and then aligning and motivating others in the fulfilment of that vision.

According to **Cohen**, "Leadership is the art of influencing others to their maximum performance to accomplish any task, objective or project."

According to **Richards** and **Engle**, "Leadership is about articulating visions, embodying values and creating an environment within which things can be accomplished."

According to **Field Marshal Mantgomery**, "Leadership is the capacity and will to rally people to a common purpose together with the character that inspires confidence and trust."

These definitions of leadership reveals that the main essence of a leader is the personality which comprises of the following elements

- **Creating** a vision for the future.
- **Inspiring and motivating** people to reach that vision.
- **Managing** by making plans for the fulfilment of that vision.
- **Building** a team to achieve that vision.

A leader, thus, has the ability to provide positive influences on the lives and behaviours of others. He/She possess the qualities that inspire, guide and mentor people in reaching a common goal.

In the field of physical education, the quality of leadership is essential not only to build a good athlete but also for the overall development of the athlete as a person.

Qualities of a Leader

A leader is a person who gathers support and cooperation from his/her colleagues, subordinates or team members. He/She possess certain qualities *i.e. personal* as well as *professional*, that are necessary in the field of physical education.

The qualities possessed by a leader includes

1. **Self Awareness** Leaders must possess a vision along with knowledge about their own strengths and weaknesses, knowledge about skills and complete information about the vision.

2. **Determination and Dedication** Leaders should have the confidence to meet the challenges with firm determination and dedication. He/She should be devoted to the profession and must be able to face even the worst situations.

3. **Intelligence** Wisdom is very important for a leader to develop intuition and insight for future events. A leader should be intelligent enough to find out all possible solutions for a complex set of problems.

4. **Strong Interpersonal Skills** A leader must be social. He/She should possess essential social qualities such as cooperation, brotherhood, sympathy, empathy, respect etc. He/She must have the ability to interact and work harmoniously with all team members.

5. **Decision-making** A leader of physical education should be able to take decision spontaneously. He/She should be able to look at the problems logically and must take decisions at the right time.

6. **Energy and Enthusiasm** A leader should be energetic and enthusiastic. He/She should be able to motivate and excite the players to give their best to the game.

7. **Good Health and High Motor Capacity** A leader in physical education should have good health and high motor fitness. He/She must display all the components of physical fitness such as strength, speed, endurance, flexibility, etc.

8. **Effective Communication Skills** Communication is an essential and integral part of positive leadership.
   A leader must be able to convey his/her thoughts and ideas clearly to the players. It plays a very effective role in teaching and coaching process.

9. **Impartiality** A good leader must be economically balanced. He/She should see everyone as equal, should be moral and should not participate in any kind of partiality.

10. **Creative** A leader in physical education must be creative. He/She must be able to produce new techniques and ideas that may be needed in this field.

11. **Teaching Skills** A leader in physical education, must have deep knowledge of various teaching skills to efficiently transfer his/her knowledge.
    He/She should also be capable of using and understanding the body language, gestures, expressions, etc.

12. **Good Personality** A leader must have a good personality. He/She should have good physical, mental and social qualities which helps to influence his/her followers.

Role of a Leader

An able leader has the capability to take his team and organisation to new heights. Thus, the role of a leader is very important in the field of physical education. Following are the main roles of a leader

1. **Guidance and Counselling** The role of a leader is to mentor as well as guide the team members and counsel them from time to time so that they do not forget the vision.
   He/She should understand his/her students and their mental needs to not only provide help but also motivate them towards achieving the personal as well as the common goal.

2. **Representation** The role of a leader is to represent the team or the organisation at different places such as in competitions, seminars, conferences etc.
   He/She is the spokesperson of the team who communicates the feelings and problems of the team to the higher authorities and works for their benefit. An effective representation increases the confidence of the entire team.

3. **Integrate Goals** The role of a leader is to integrate the individual goals with that of the organisation or team. In this way, a leader brings people closer to work for a common goal or a common purpose.

4. **Support and Cooperation** The leader, with his intelligence, maturity and pleasing personality, helps the team members by providing them support and increasing cooperation.
   He/She leads all the matters related to discipline and settles all the internal differences. He/She controls the internal relationship within a team and makes all efforts to raise the morale of the team.

5. **Decision Maker** The role of a leader is to take strategic decisions for the success of the team as well as develop plans to realise those decisions.

6. **Team Builder** An important role is to make an impressive team that consists of people with different talents so that the team members assist each other instead of competing with each other.

7. **Organiser** A good leader in sports is also a good organiser. He/She not only organises any group event that may take place, but also plan the ways in which a team/athlete may achieve its goal. He/She has a thorough and vivid knowledge to lay out the plan.

8. **Executor** A good leader makes sure that the plans are executed well. It is his/her responsibility to make sure that the objectives of the group are put well into all the affairs. He/she makes sure that the execution take place efficiently and with care.

9. **Examplary** A good leader acts as an example for his/her team. He/She sets up an example of top norms of conduct, character and idealism. He/She shows all those qualities within himself/herself that he/she wants his/her team to gain or learn.

Adventure Sports

Adventure sports also called as *action sports*, *aggro sports* and *extreme sports* is a popular term for certain activities perceived as having a high level of inherent danger. These activities are usually outdoor sports which involves certain intense actions involving speed, height, etc., that creates an adventurous atmosphere.

In these games, sports person go through unlimited thrill, excitement, entertainment and adventure.

Generally, adventure sports can be understood as the sports that involve extraordinary speed, scaling height, physical exertion and sometimes life-threatening stunts. However, a very clear and precise definition of the term has yet not been found.

According to **Dr. Rhonda Cohen**, "An adventure sport is a competitive (comparison or self-evaluative) activity within which the participant is subjected to natural or unusual physical and mental challenges such as speed, height, depth or natural forces and where fast and accurate cognitive perceptual processing may be required for a successful outcome."

As explained by the **Living Dangerously Website**, the phrases 'adventure sport' or 'extreme sport' are used to classify certain activities that feature a high level of danger. According to them, "These activities often involve speed, height, a high level of physical exertion, and high specialised gear or spectacular stunts."

Adventure sports have been best defined as "Outdoor sports or activities in which the participants competes in a natural environment, more against themselves than against others."

Objectives of Adventure Sports

The main aim and objectives of adventure sports is to provide a carefully planned stimulating environment which will help each individual achieve excellent foundation for creative learning and independence.

As adventure sport is more of an individual sport rather than a team sport, it essentially focuses on the development and growth of an individual.

Its objectives are as follows

1. **To Develop Self-confidence** By overcoming the fear and experiencing the thrill, one can develop self-confidence. Individuals who participate in adventure sports compete against themselves and therefore have a great sense of achievement when they reach their goal.

2. **To Build the Concentration** In these sports, a person has to be very alert and attentive all the time.

   Hence, a person develops a habit of extended attention and concentration.

3. **To Develop Mental and Physical Fitness** Adventure sports involves fitness skills like jumping, climbing, swimming, etc. These activities then help in building mental and physical fitness.

4. **To Improve Social Relations** During participation in adventure sports, qualities like sympathy cooperation, helpfulness, adjustment, sincerity, patience, are developed between two individuals.

5. **To Have a Bond with Nature** Most of the adventure sports are outdoor activities which give enough opportunities to experience nature. A result of this exposure to nature, makes an individual bond with the nature so that he/she not only learns to respect it but also learns to cherish it.

6. **To Face the Challenges Against any Odd Situations** These sports enhance one's capacity to face odd situations with courage and determination.

7. **Proper Use of Abundant Energy** Adventure sports provide the participants a positive and a healthy channelisation of their energy and enthusiasm. Such use of energy is beneficial for the holistic development of the individual.

8. **To Provide Amusement and Excitement** It is the vital objective of adventure sports to provide amusement, excitement, exhilaration, recreation, and enjoyment.

Types of Adventure Sports

Various types of adventure sports are as follows

Rock Climbing

Rock climbing is an activity in which participants climb up, down or across natural rock formations or artificial rock walls.

The goal is to reach the summit of a formation or the end point of a pre-defined route without falling. To successfully complete a climb, one must return to the base of the route safely.

As one of the most dangerous adventurous sports, rock climbing requires strong mental control, agility, flexibility, endurance and various coordinative abilities such as coordination, balance, etc.

For the safe and secure completion of routes, knowledge of proper equipments and its usage along with climbing techniques is must. Even with utmost care, it is an accident prone sport.

Due to the length and extended endurance required in the sport, accidents are more likely to happen on descent than on ascent, especially on the larger multiple patches.

Apart from being an entertaining sport, various rock climbing competitions are also organised all around the world.

These competitions have the objective of either completing the route in the quickest possible time or attaining the farthest point on an increasingly difficult route.

Further, because of the wide range and variety of rock formations around the world, rock climbing has been separated into several different styles and kinds, such as aid climbing, free climbing, bouldering, free soloing, top rope climbing, trad climbing, sport climbing, etc.

Safety Measures During Rock Climbing

The following safety measures should be taken before and while taking part in this activity

- Don't climb higher than you are supposed to.
- Put the harness on the body correctly, so that you do not get tangled in the rope if you fall.
- If you are new to rock climbing, belay (*i.e.* fix a running rope round a rock to secure it) with an experienced climber.
- Use the right equipment like shoes, ropes, slings, etc.
- Practise falling away from the rock wall (so you do not hit any rocks on the way down). You will fall sometimes, especially if you want to get better.
- Take small breaks in between attempts. Give yourself a chance to recover before climbing again.
- Practise correct technique. Many new climbers try to hang with their fingers and elbow; this technique wastes energy and isn't effective.
  Your arms should be used for shifting weight, not trying to hold yourself up with a tight grip.
- Watch experienced climbers to help you improve your own technique and climbing safety.

Trekking

Trekking can be defined as a form of walking, undertaken with the specific purpose of exploring and enjoying the scenery.

It is essentially a long walking journey that usually takes place on trails in areas of relatively unspoiled wilderness, especially the mountains.

In other words, trekking is a journey on foot to remote regions where there may be no proper road and modes of transport.

It is to be kept in mind that trekking is not an easy task to do. Infact, it requires a lot of courage and confidence alongwith a strong physique.

It is also known as **backpacking** in America, **Trumping** in New Zealand and **Hiking** in India.

Trekking involves carrying bag with all the things that may be required for a journey of more than a day. This can include food, water, bedding, shelter, clothing, stove, cooking kit, etc.

Trekking is all about enjoying a great walking holiday of either overnight hikes or extended hikes of many days.

As a physical sport, it helps not only in building self-confidence but also improves the general health of an individual, especially the cardiovascular system.

Types of Trekking

Based on its difficulty level, trekking may be of four types which are as follows

1. **Easy Trekking** This kind of trekking is generally done by beginners. It does not include any kind of difficult high-altitude climbing. In other words, it includes easy climbing.
2. **Moderate Trekking** Treks that are slightly difficult and challenging, come under this category. It requires more energetic climbers, as it usually takes longer than 10 days of walking up and down.
3. **Strenuous Trekking** This type of trekking needs a lot of physical effort, energy and determination. Such trekking requires a previous experience in mountain walking, as treks involve walking to high altitude about 5,000 m.
4. **Difficult Trekking** This is the type of trekking that includes walking up to some very steep altitudes. The participants of this kind of trekking must have enough experience as well as endurance to take this trek, as it generally extends over one month.

Safety Measures During Trekking

The following safety measures should be taken before and while taking part in this activity

- Avoid trekking during the rainy season or during bad weather. Before starting, check the weather report for the area where you are going and prepare yourself or your group (if any) accordingly.
- Take all the required materials like water, matchbox, food items, rope, sleeping bag, tent, etc.
- To avoid insect bites, wear full sleeve shirts and full pants.
- Wear proper footwear so that you do not slip while trekking in hilly areas. Do not eat leaves, flowers etc. found on the wayside, as they may be poisonous.
- Take along a multi-pocket carry bag which is large enough to carry all the essential items.
- It is suggested that you use trekking stick for better and efficient trekking.

River Rafting

River rafting or white water rafting is the challenging recreational outdoor activity of using an inflatable raft to navigate a river or any other water body.

This is often done on 'white water' (meaning different degrees of rough and harshly flowing water), in order to thrill and excite the passengers on the raft.

This activity as a leisure sport, became popular in the mid-1970s, evolving from individuals paddling 3 metre rafts with double-bladed paddles to multi-person rafts propelled by single-bladed paddles and steered by a tour guide at the stern. It is considered an extreme sport and can even be fatal.

The modern raft is an inflatable boat consisting of very durable, multilayered rubberised (hypalon) or vinyl (PVC) fabric with several independent air chambers.

It is usually propelled with ordinary paddles and typically holds 4 to 12 persons.

Rafts come in different forms like

- A symmetrical raft steered with a double-bladed paddle at the stern, which is the most common one used in Europe and Australia.
- An asymmetrical rudder-controlled raft.
- A symmetrical raft with central helm (oars) and stern mounts with the oar frame located at the rear of the raft.

Based on how demanding the paths of the rivers are, river rafting has been classified into grades ranging from I to VI. These are as follows

- **Grade I** The river has flat water but potentially with small waves. The path is clear of obstacles, or has very few obstacles to manoeuvre around. This type is generally enjoyed by the beginners.
- **Grade II** The river may have some waves or rough water with little obstruction in the form of rocks. It require guidance for safe navigation.
- **Grade III** It is the most common route including normal waves, rocks with a clear passage downstream. However, careful manoeuvring, prior experience and strong paddling skills under an experienced guide are required.
- **Grade IV** The river has many irregular sized large waves and obstacles including rocks. This grade should not be performed without any prior experience and the presence of an experienced guide.
- **Grade V** The rivers have large and irregular waves, with many obstructions in the forms of large rocks. It requires very careful and précise manoeuvring. Only the individuals with advanced training and experience should participate at this level.

- **Grade VI** The river has huge waves. This level is very tough and thus requires great physical endurance and mental toughness. At this level, the individuals may face any injury or even death.

Safety Measures During River Rafting

The following safety measures should be taken before and while taking part in this activity

- Never go on this activity alone. Always have a team of people in the raft.
- All participants must have adequate capabilities as swimmers, in case of an accident.
- Always wear a life vest and helmet while participating in this activity.
- Before starting, check all the equipments to ensure everything is okay. Particularly check the dinghy / raft for any cracks and proper air level.
- If any participant feels tired, he should not drag his paddle in the water, as it might hit a rock in the river.
- Drink plenty of liquids before, during and after the rafting activity, as this activity makes you dehydrated.
- End your rafting before darkness falls; if it is getting dark, don't go for this activity.

Mountaineering

Mountaineering, also referred to as 'mountain climbing' or 'Alpinism' in Europe, is the sport of climbing or ascending a high mountain.

Often confused with rock climbing and hiking, mountaineering differs from these sports. This adventurous sport is a combination of the skills required in hiking as well as rock climbing.

Also, the mountains generally have a mixed terrain with the presence of rock, ice and snow, so climbers need to be able to navigate through a wide variety of conditions.

Depending on the case, mountaineering may involve using technical equipment and combining a series of related skills.

Climbing mountains embodies the thrills produced by testing one's courage, resourcefulness, strength, ability, and stamina to the utmost in a situation of inherent risk. In fact, this adventurous sports challenges an individual's capabilities and skills.

Besides reaching a summit, the main objective of a mountaineering trip lies on overcoming safely every hazard along the route.

For most climbers, the pleasures of mountaineering lie not only in the 'conquest' of a peak but also in the physical and spiritual satisfactions brought about through intense personal effort, ever-increasing proficiency, and contact with natural grandeur.

Safety Measures During Mountaineering

The following safety measures should be taken before and while taking part in this activity

- Before each excursion, look at the latest weather forecast for the area and keep your eye open for any changes in the weather.
- Assess your fitness level objectively and choose a suitable mountain to climb.
- Before starting, check all the equipment to ensure everything is okay, particularly the safety equipment, like ropes and slings, climbing boots, protective clothes for cold weather etc.

Surfing

Surfing is a surface water sport in which the wave rider, referred to as a surfer, rides on the forward part or face of a moving wave on the surface of the water, which is usually carrying the surfer towards the shore.

In other words, a surfer waits for an ocean, river or man-made wave and then glides across the wave until it breaks and loses its energy.

The ultimate goal of surfing is to ride and progress with a moving wave using a surfboard.

According to many historians, surfing had been a sport in Hawaii, even before Christopher Columbus sailed in 1942. These ancient surfers generally used wooden boards that were up to 18 feet (5.5 m long).

Today, surfing is a popular adventurous sport in many countries including Australia, Brazil, France, etc.

The boards used for surfing today are made of a strong, lightweight plastic called polyurethane and fibreglass.

These boards fall under two categories

1. **Short Board** Board under the length of 7 feet (2 m) with a width of about 20 inches (51 cm) and a thickness of 2 inches (5 cm) is called short board. It weighs from 6-8 pounds (2.5-3.5 kgs).
2. **Long Board** Board with the length of more than 7 feet with a width of 23 inches (5.8 cm) and a thickness of 2.5 inches (6 cm) is called long board. It weighs from 15-17 pounds (7-8 kgs).

All forms of surfing requires sharp reflexes to stay balanced. Surfers should be able to anticipate what breaking a wave will do. Many surfers train their bodies by running and body building for the different categories of surfing.

Types of Surfing

The various categories of surfing are as follows

1. **Stand-up Surfing** The modern-day definition of surfing most often refers to stand-up surfing. In this, a surfer rides a wave by standing up on a surfboard. It is the most popular and easiest method of surfing.
2. **Body Boarding** In this form of surfing, a surfer rides a wave on a body board (full body length board), either lying on the belly, on a dropped knee, or standing up.
3. **Knee Boarding** This is a type of surfing done from a kneeling position, usually on a small, wide, blunt-nosed board. People doing this form of surfing prefer it because of the increased sensation of speed that comes from riding closer to the water surface.
4. **Surf Matting** This is also called Mat surfing. It is a type of surfing performed on a soft, inflatable, rectangular surf mat consisting of four pontoons stuck together. It is suitable for beginners, so children start learning surfing with it.
5. **Body Surfing** In this, the wave is surfed without a board, using the surfer's own body to catch and ride the wave. It is considered by some to be the purest form of surfing, but it is the most difficult form which requires much practice.
6. **Tow-in Surfing** In this, a motorised boat tows the surfer into the wave front, helping the surfer match a large wave's speed, which is generally a higher speed than what a self-propelled surfer can produce. Thus, it is the safest form of surfing for beginners.

Safety Measures During Surfing

The following safety measures should be taken before and while taking part in this activity

- Make sure you warm up before surfing. This may include a general body warm-up followed by suitable stretches.
- Take lessons from an approved surfing training agency to learn appropriate skills, techniques and water safety if you haven't surfed before.
- Use the correct surfing equipment, like a surfboard with nose guards (to minimise injury risk) and a wetsuit for buoyancy, sun protection and to prevent any injuries.
- Follow surfing etiquette, meaning that respect the rights of other surfers in the water. There is not enough room on a wave for more than one surfer; otherwise collisions, injury and conflict between surfers can occur.

Paragliding

Paragliding is the recreational and competitive adventure sport of flying paragliders *i.e.* a lightweight, free-flying, foot-launched glider aircraft with no rigid primary structure.

A paraglider is a foot launched, ram air, airfoil canopy that is flown and landed solely on the energy of the wind, gravity and the pilot's muscle power.

In other words, the pilot or the individual is suspended through a harness attached to a fabric that acts like a wing.

Wing shape is maintained by the suspension lines, the pressure of air entering vents in the front of the wing, and the aerodynamic forces of the air flowing over the outside.

This sport consists of only 3 equipments, *i.e.* the harness, a wing and a helmet that weighs less than 20 kgs, which can be easily packed into a bag and carried around.

Despite not using an engine, paraglider flight can even last many hours and cover many hundreds of kilometres (in rare cases), though flights of one to two hours and covering some tens of kilometres are normal.

By skilful exploitation of sources of lift, the pilot may gain height, often climbing to altitudes of a few thousand metres.

Safety Measures During Paragliding

The following safety measures should be taken before and while taking part in this activity

- Practise for increasing endurance and physical strength, as it will make the sport more enjoyable for you.
- Enhance your ability by taking your glider to a field and work on your ground handling.
- Gain knowledge about techniques by searching websites, reading blogs as well as books on the sport. They will give you knowledge about the basics, flying, weather and also about first aid.
- Weather is the most important constraint to manage even for people with a high level of experience. It is always important to watch the forecast from a reliable source before leaving for paragliding.
  Wind is the main factor and a strong and straight wind can turn out to be very disastrous.
- Look for a good paragliding site. Visibility and accessibility of the site are important. Irregular and rough landings may lead to fractured bones.
- Go for paragliding spots with visible wind indicators to assist you on which direction to take.

Safety Measures to Prevent Sports Injuries

Sports is one of the most effective physical activities that provide innumerable health benefits. It improves physical coordination, fitness, mood, sleep habits, etc.

It also helps in reducing stress and depression, boosting your self-confidence and maintaining a healthy weight.

There are so many choices of sports that one can choose from like basketball, football, baseball, volleyball, badminton, etc.

However, as human beings, we are not immune to certain injuries. While participating in sports or games, an individual is always at risk of sport injuries.

Hence, ensuring safety is essential in preventing any sports related injury. It is important that we take care of our body in performing sports and even fitness-related activities.

There are various tips or methods that help in preventing any sport injuries.

These tips or methods are as follows

1. **Wear Protective Gear** One cannot tell if he/she will encounter accidents or emergencies in the middle of the game. Hence, he/she should always be ready. Wear protective gears, equipment, and devices that will protect him/her from unexpected injuries.

   This includes mouth guards, helmets, gloves, protective pads, proper shoes and other equipment. Also, he/she should make sure to wear equipment suited to his/her age.

2. **Warm-up** Warming-up is a must before engaging into sports. It prepares the body, mind, and heart for the training or the sports. Warming-up gradually raises the heart rate, warms muscles and connective tissues, improves the mobility and promotes functionality of all individuals' body movements.

   It also allows entry of oxygen to the muscles, tendons, ligaments and flexible joints which reduces the risk of injury.

3. **Take Rest** It is extremely important that one should always listen to his/her body. When he/she engage in sports, he/she must remember that learning or training is a slow process. Fatigue often lead to sports injuries. Hence, take breaks and give the body proper rest.

4. **Improve Technique** Based on the principles of biomechanics, the most effective way of improving oneself performance is by improving his/her techniques.

   His/Her physical built is just a small factor in his/her performance. The coordination of his/her body movements is important in performing well in different kinds of sports.

5. **Keep Hydrated** Our body is composed of 60% of water. When we exercise or we do sports, we lose this water in the form of prespiration. Thus, we need to gain this water through proper hydration.

   According to sports dietitians, water is essential in maintaining blood volume, regulating body temperature and allowing muscle contractions. Apart from water, hydrating drinks that are rich in electrolytes are recommended for athletes.

6. **Cool Down** If warming-up is important, cooling down is also essential. After working out or training, you have to spend at least 10 minutes of performing gentle exercises that will return your heart rate to a normal pace.

   By cooling down, you are allowing your body to remove excess wastes and allow the flow of oxygen and nutrients into your muscles.

7. **Know the Rules of the Game** You need to have proper knowledge of the mechanics and rules of the sports. These rules are made to prevent athletes from acquiring injuries.

8. **Eat Healthy** Diet and proper nutrition are important for athletes. A good nutrition plan is the foundation of an effective fitness program.

   The demands of sports and exercise on the body mean that you should replace all the energy and nutrients consumed by eating healthy food.

   For athletes, it is important that they eat regular, well-balanced meals to fuel their training or sport. They should also take protein to promote muscle health.

Chapter Practice

Objective Questions

• Multiple Choice Questions

1. Which of the following is not an element of leadership?
(a) Creating   (b) Managing
(c) Building   (d) Teaching

Ans. (d) Teaching is not an element of leadership. Leaders create new ideas, manage people and build relations with team members.

2. Which of the following is not a quality of a leader?
(a) Good personality
(b) Pride
(c) Passion, determination and dedication
(d) Good communication skills

Ans. (b) Pride is not a quality of a leader. Leaders should have attractive personality, they should be dedicated and determined. They should have good communication skills.

3. Arun is made the group leader of a mountaineering expedition. On the first day he told about all the group activities to his team. Arun and his group members executed all the plans nicely.

Which among the following is the role of a leader?
(a) Planning for the group
(b) Logical decision making
(c) Be a representative of his team
(d) All of the above

Ans. (d) The role of a leader is to make plans for the whole group, to take logical decisions on behalf of the group and the leader is also a representative of his team. So, Arun is a good group leader.

4. The main objective of adventure sports is
(a) To carefully provide an environment that helps an individual to create a base for learning and independence.
(b) To develop self worth and self confidence while being in the lap of nature.
(c) To aid a holistic development of an individual.
(d) To direct the abundant energy towards a proper aim.

Ans. (a) The main objective of adventure sports is to carefully provide an environment that helps an individual to create a base for learning and independence.

5. Which safety measure is used for the adventure sport shown in the below image?

(a) Fix a running rope
(b) Do not eat wayside leaves or flowers
(c) Always wear a life jacket
(d) Keep close watch on visible wind indicators

Ans. (a) Fixing a running rope around the waist of the climber is a safety measure used for this adventure sport.

6. Adventure sports are activities that are risky and involve some sort of danger. They are performed in natural environment and do not harm the nature. These type of sports have become very popular.

Which of the following is not an adventure sports?
(a) Handball   (b) Scuba diving
(c) Skiing   (d) Rock climbing

Ans. (a) Handball is not an adventure sport. It is played by two teams. Scuba diving, skiing and rock climbing are adventure sports.

7. In rock climbing, the hands serve the purpose of
(a) hanging properly
(b) being stable while holding the rocks
(c) shifting weight
(d) None of the above

Ans. (c) In rock climbing, the hands serve the purpose of shifting weight.

8. You and your friends planned for camping to countryside near a lake. You have carefully planned for the outing and packed all the essentials.

Which of the following is not an equipment needed for trekking?
(a) Sleeping bag
(b) Ropes
(c) Surfing board
(d) Mountain axe

Ans. (c) Surfing board is not an equipment needed for trekking. Sleeping bag, ropes and mountain axe may be required in it but surfing board is not needed in trekking.

9. River rafting is divided into grades on the basis of
(a) roughness of river
(b) type of boat
(c) level of experience of participants
(d) None of the above

Ans. (a) River rafting is divided into grades on the basis of roughness of river. i.e. some where the river water flows slowly and some where it is very fast.

10. What is the European name of the sport shown in the image below?

(a) Rock climbing
(b) Alpinism
(c) Mountaineering
(d) Surf Mating

Ans. (b) The European name of the sports shown in the image is Alpinism as Alps mountains are present in Europe. Mountaineering is done on these mountains.

11. Identify the adventure sports shown in the image.

(a) Trekking
(b) Rock Climbing
(c) Surfing
(d) River Rafting

Ans. (c) The adventure sports shown in the image is surfing. It is a water sport.

12. The pilot or the individual is suspended through a harness attached to a fabric that acts like a wing. Wing shape is maintained by the suspension lines. The sport consist of only three equipments i.e, the harness, a wing and a helmet.

The adventure sport that is described here is...........
(a) Surfing
(b) Sky diving
(c) Paragliding
(d) Sailing

Ans. (c) The adventure sport that is described here is paragliding. It is a recreational and competitive adventure sport.

13. Match the following.

	List I		List II
A.	Moderate trekking	1.	Experienced trekkers
B.	Difficult trekking	2.	Beginners
C.	Easy trekking	3.	Trekkers with experience and endurance
D.	Strenuous trekking	4.	Energetic trekkers

	A	B	C	D		A	B	C	D
(a)	4	3	2	1	(b)	1	4	3	2
(c)	3	1	4	2	(d)	4	2	1	3

Ans. (a) The correct match is A-4, B-3, C-2 and D-1.

14. Match the following.

	List I		List II
A.	River Rafting	1.	Climbing boots
B.	Paragliding	2.	Life Jacket
C.	Mountaineering	3.	Helmet
D.	Surfing	4.	Body suit (wet)

	A	B	C	D		A	B	C	D
(a)	1	4	2	3	(b)	3	1	4	2
(c)	2	3	1	4	(d)	4	1	2	3

Ans. (c) The correct match is A-2, B-3, C-1 and D-4.

• Assertion and Reasoning

Directions (Q. Nos. 1-4) *Each of these questions contains two statements, Assertion (A) and Reason (R). Each of these questions also has four alternative choices, any one of which is the correct answer. You have to select one of the codes (a), (b), (c) and (d) given below.*

Codes
(a) Both A and R are true and R is the correct explanation of A
(b) Both A and R are true, but R is not the correct explanation of A
(c) A is true, but R is false
(d) A is false, but R is true

1. Assertion (A) Leadership is a unique skill that cannot be taught but can be learned through observing others.

Reason (R) Every individual has leadership quality.

Ans. (c) The assertion is true as leadership can be learnt by observing others. It is a skill that is acquired. Reason is false as every person do not have leadership qualities. Thus, A is true, but R is false.

2. Assertion (A) A leader has a capacity to change the society.

Reason (R) Leaders helps in guiding people on the right path.

Ans. (a) Assertion is true as a leader has power and the ability by which he can make followers. Thus, he can change the society. Reason is true as leaders also act as guide to show the right path to the people. Reason correctly explains assertion. Thus, both A and R are true and R is the correct explanation of A.

3. Assertion (A) A good leader in sports is also a good organiser.

Reason (R) The role of a leader is to integrate the individual goal with that of the organisation or team.

Ans. (b) Assertion is true as a good leader organises the activities also so leader is an organiser too. Reason is also true as a true leader integrates individual goals with that of the team or organisation. Reason donot explains assertion. Thus, both A and R are true, but R is not the correct explanation of A.

4. Assertion (A) Adventure games do not improve social relation.

Reason (R) Surfing is a famous adventure game.

Ans. (d) Assertion is false as adventure games actually improves social relation. It helps in mixing with people. Reason is true as surfing is a famous adventure sports. It is done on waves. Thus, A is false, but R is true.

● Case Based MCQs

1. The main aim of physical eduction is overall development of a student. Through the participation in physical education programmes, the qualities of a student can be developed. Organising trips, camps and similar activities in natural environment helps in developing the latent abilities in students.

(i) Which of the following takes place through physical education?

(a) Growth   (b) Development

(c) Emotional stability   (d) All of these

Ans. (d) Through physical education, proper growth and development of a person along with emotional stablity takes place in an individual.

(ii) Physical education helps in developing which of the following qualities?

(a) Determination

(b) Intelligence

(c) Dedication

(d) All of these

Ans. (d) Physical education helps in developing the qualities of determination, intelligence, dedication etc. It makes a person physically and mentally strong.

(iii) Camping is part of which adventure sports?

(a) Trekking   (b) Surfing

(c) Paragliding   (d) All of these

Ans. (a) Camping is part of the adventure sports 'trekking'. In trekking, people walk for long distances.

2. Surfing is a sport of riding on the waves in the standing position. Sometimes surfers like to surf in lying position also. Raman is a surfer, he has done surfing in the Arabian sea. Now, he is a lifeguard on the beach and also coaches young surfers. Based on this information answer the following questions.

(i) Which of the following is a necessary item needed for surfing?

(a) Wet suit   (b) Sun glasses

(c) Paddle raft   (d) Helmet

Ans. (a) Wet suit is a necessary item needed for surfing. It provides protection while wet.

(ii) The surf board is made up of which material?

(a) Iron   (b) Aluminium

(c) Fibreglass   (d) Thick cloth

Ans. (c) The surf board is made up of fibreglass. It is very lightweight and strong material.

(iii) Surfing activity can be done in _________ .

(a) Oceans

(b) Seas

(c) Rivers

(d) All of the above

Ans. (d) Surfing can be done in oceans, seas or rivers. Thus, option (d) is the correct answer.

Subjective Questions

• Short Answer (SA) Type Questions

1. What is the importance of leadership in sports?

Ans. Leadership is referred to as the activity of inspiring people to perform and engage in achieving a goal. In sports, leadership is very important because sports requires a clear objective, a definite goal and team spirit.

A person with leadership skills builds a strong team and gives a clear vision which helps the teammates to focus on the target.

Creating a clear vision helps to fix a definite goal and achieve it. For instance, in a hockey match, leadership skills shown by the team captain will help the team to focus on scoring goals and achieving success.

2. Why are strong interpersonal skills required in a leader?

Ans. In terpersonal skills means the ability to communicate and interact well with people. For a leader, it is important to process strong interpersonal skills so that there is proper interaction with the other members of his team.

This helps in increasing cooperation, building support and motivating teammates. A leader has to work harmoniously with others; for that effective communication is needed. A leader with strong interpersonal skills brings success for his team.

3. Briefly explain any three objectives of adventure sports.

Ans. Three objectives of adventure sports are as follows

    (i) **To develop Mental and Physical Fitness** Adventure sports involves fitness skills like jumping, climbing and swimming etc. These activities thus help us building mental and physical fitness.

    (ii) **To Improve Social Relations** During participation in adventure sports, qualities like sympathy cooperation, helpfulness, adjustment, sincerity, patience, are developed between two individuals.

    (iii) **To Provide Amusement and Excitement** It is the vital objective of adventure sports to provide amusement, excitement, exhilaration, recreation and enjoyment.

4. Enlist the safety measures that should be taken while rock climbing.

Ans. The safety measures that should be taken while rock climbing are as follows

- Don't climb higher than you are supposed to.
- Put the harness on the body correctly, so that you do not get tangled in the rope if you fall.
- If you are new to rock climbing, belay (i.e., fix a running rope round a rock to secure it) with an experienced climber.
- Use the right equipment like shoes, ropes, slings etc.
- Practise falling away from the rock wall (so you do not hit any rocks on the way down). You will fall sometimes, especially if you want to get better.

5. Define rock climbing. Why is it considered as a dangerous sport?

Ans. Rock climbing is an activity in which participants climb up, down or across natural rock formations or artificial rock walls with the objective of reaching the summit of a formation or the end point of a pre-defined route without falling.

Rock climbing is considered a dangerous sport because knowledge of proper climbing teachniques and usage of specialised climbing equipment is crucial for the safe completion of routes.

The duration and length of climb may be too tiring and high level of endurance is required otherwise it may lead to acidents.

6. Differentiate between rock climbing and trekking on basis of their nature.

Ans. The differences between rock climbing and trekking are as follows

Rock Climbing	Trekking
Rock climbing is an activity in which participants climb up, down or across natural rock formation or artificial rockwalls.	Trekking is a form of walk, undertaken with the specific purpose of exploring and enjoying the scenery.
The goal is to reach the summit of a formation or the end point of a pre-defined route without falling.	It involves carrying bag with all the things that may be required for a journey of more than a day.
This activity can be done only after practice as it involves climbing techniques.	This can be done by anyone even old people as it involves walking.

7. What are the safety measures that should be used while trekking?

Ans. The following safety measures should be used in trekking

- Avoid trekking during the rainy season or during bad weather. Before starting, check the weather report for the area where you are going and prepare yourself accordingly.

- Take all the required materials like water, matchbox, food items, rope, sleeping bags, etc.
- To avoid insect bites, wear full sleeve shirts and full pants.
- Wear proper footwear so that you do not slip while trekking in hilly areas.
- Do not eat leaves, flowers etc found on the wayside, as they may be poisonous.
- Take along a multi-pocket carry bag which is large enough to carry all the essential items.

8. What are the different types of raft used in river rafting? Also describe the modern raft.

Ans. Three different types of rafts are used in river rafting. They are as follows
- A symmetrical raft with a double bladed paddle.
- A symmetrical rudder-controlled raft
- A symmetrical raft with central helm and the stern mounted with the oar frame located at the rear of the raft.

Three modern raft used in river rafting is an inflatable boat consisting of very durable, multilayered rubberised (hypalon or vinyl) PVC fabric with several independent air chambers. It is usually propelled with ordinary paddles and typically holds 4 to 12 persons.

9. Write a short note on the adventure sports of mountaineering.

Ans. Mountaineering, also referred to as 'mountain climbing' or 'Alpinism' in Europe, is the sport of climbing or ascending a high mountain.

Often confused with rock climbing and hiking, mountaineering differs from these sports. The adventurous sport is a combination of the skills required in hiking as well as rock climbing.

Also, the mountains generally have a mixed terrian with the presence of rock, ice and snow, so climbers need to be able to nevigate through a wide variety of conditions.

Besides reaching a summit, the main objective of a mountaineering trip lies on overcoming safely every hazard along the route.

Depending on the case, mountaineering involves using technical equipment and combining a series of related skills.

It test one's courage, resourcefulness, cunning, strength, ability and stamina to the utmost in a situation of inherent risk.

10. What safety measures should be followed while mountaineering?

Ans. The safety measures followed while mountaineering are as follows

Before each excursion, look at the latest weather forcast for the area and keep close watch on local weather changes.

Check all the equipments, ropes, slings, boots, protective clothes and gears. They should be in proper condition.

Eat right amount of food and monitor your fitness levels before starting any mountaineering expedition.

Put on proper warm clothes and shoes according to the terrain.

Carry some high energy giving foods and water.

Drink plenty of liquids to avoid dehydration.

11. What should be the dimensions of long and short boards in surfing?

Ans. The longboards used in surfing have a length of more than 7 feet. Its width should be 23 inches (58 cm) and the thickness of 2.5 inches (6 cm). The average weight of a long board should be 15-17 pounds (7-8 kg).

The short board used in surfing should have a length of 7 feet (2 m), width of about 20 inches (51 cm) and a thickness of 2 inches (5 cm). The short board should weigh from 6 to 8 pounds (2.5 – 3.5 kgs). Both long and short boards are made up of strong but lightweight plastic called fibreglass or polyurethane.

12. Enlist three safety measures while surfing.

Ans. Surfing is a surface water sport in which the wave rider, referred to as a surfer, rides on the forward part or face of a moving wave on the surface of the water, which is usually carrying the surfer towards the shore.

The three safety measures are as follows
(i) Use the correct equipment like surfboard with nose guards, a wetsuit for buoyancy, sun protection etc.
(ii) Take lessons from an approved trainer, agency to learn appropriate lessons, skills and techniques.
(iii) Warm up before starting to surf. Do body warm up exercises.

13. What are the distances and durations which paragliders normally fly before landing? By what techniques can they extend these distances and times?

Ans. Paragliders normally fly for one to two hours and cover tens of kilometres before landing despite not using an engine.

By skillful exploitation of lift, the pilot of the paraglider may gain height, often climbing to altitudes of a few thousand metres so that the flight can even last many hours and cover many hundreds of kilometres (in rare cases).

As wind is the main factor here, paragliders can identify the direction of the wind and sail accordingly.

● Long Answer (LA) Type Questions

1. Explain in detail six qualities a leader should possess.

Ans. The qualities which a leader should possess are as follows

  (i) **Self-awareness** Leaders must possess vision along with knowledge about their own strengths and weaknesses, knowledge about skills and complete information about the vision.

  (ii) **Determination and Dedication** Leaders should have the confidence to meet the challenges with firm determination and dedication. He/She should be devoted to the profession and must be able to face even the worst situations.

  (iii) **Intelligence** Wisdom is very important for a leader to develop intuition and insight for future events.

  A leader should be intelligent enough to find out all possible solutions for a complex set of problems.

  (iv) **Strong Interpersonal Skills** A leader must be social. He/She should possess essential social qualities such as cooperation, affections, brotherhood, sympathy, empathy, respect etc.

  He/She must have the ability to interact and work harmoniously with all team members.

  (v) **Decision Making** A leader of physical education should be able to take decision spontaneously.

  He/She should be able to look at the problems logically and must take decisions at the right time.

  (vi) **Energy and Enthusiasm** A leader should be energetic and enthusiastic. He/She should be able to motive and excite the players to give their best to the game.

2. Decribe the role of a leader in the success of his/her team.

Ans. A leader has immense responsibility for his team. A leader is a guide, a counsellor, a supporter, a team builder and a representative of his/her team. A leader is also a major decisions maker.

The role of a leader is as follows

  (i) **Guidance and Counselling** The role of a leader is to mentor or guide the team members and counsel them from time to time so that they do not forget the vision.

  (ii) **Representation** The role of a leader is to represent the team or the organisation at different places such as in competitions, seminars, conferences etc.

  He/She is the spokesperson of the team who communicates their feelings and problems to the higher authorities and works for their benefit.

  An effective representation increases the confidence of the entire team.

  (iii) **Integrate Goals** The role of a leader is to integrate the individual goals with that of the organisation or team. In this way, a leader brings people closer to work for a common goal or a common purpose.

  (iv) **Support and Cooperation** The leader, with his intelligence, maturity and pleasing personality, helps the team members by providing them support and increasing cooperation.

  He/She deals with matters related to disciplines and settles all internal differences. He/She controls internal relationships and increases the morale of the team.

  (v) **Decision Maker** The role of a leader is to make strategic decisions for the success of the team as well as develop plans to realise those decisions.

  (vi) **Team Builder** An important role of a leader is to make an impressive team that consists of people with different talents so that the team members assist each other instead of competing with each other.

3. Explain how the adventure sport of river rafting is carried out. Why is it considered an extreme sport?

Ans. River rafting or white water rafting is the challenging recreational outdoor activity of using an inflatable raft to navigate a river or other water body.

This is often done on white water (meaning different degrees or rough water), in order to thrill and excite the passengers on the raft.

This activity as a leisure sport has became popular in the mid-1970s, evolving from individuals padding 3 metre long rafts with double bladed paddles to multi person rafts propelled by single bladed paddles and steered by a tour guide at the stern.

The modern raft is an inflatable boat consisting of very durable, multilayered rubberised (hypalon) or vinyl (PVC) fabric with several independent air chambers. It is usually propelled with ordinary paddles and typically propelled with ordinary paddles and typically holds 4 to 12 persons.

Extreme sports are recreational activities perceived as involving a high degree of risk. These activities often involve speed, height, a high level of physical exertion and highly specialised gear. As river rafting meets all these conditions, it is considered an extreme sports.

4. What is surfing? Explain any five types of surfing in detail.

Ans. Surfing is a surface water sport in which the wave rider, referred to as surfer, rides on the forward or deep face of a moving wave on the surface of the water, which usually carries the surfer towards the shore. Five types of surfing are as follows

  (i) **Stand-up Surfing** The modern-day definition of surfing most often refers to stand up surfing. In this, a surfer rides a wave by standing up on a surfboard. It is the most popular and easiest method of surfing.

(ii) **Body Boarding** In this form of surfing, a surfer rides a wave on a body board (full body length board), either lying on the belly, on a dropped knee, or standing up.

(iii) **Knee Boarding** This is a type of surfing done from a kneeling position, usually on a small, wide, blunt-nosed board. People doing this form of surfing prefer it because of the increased sensation of speed that comes from riding closer to the water surface.

(iv) **Surf Matting** This is also called Mat surfing. It is a type of surfing performed on a soft, inflatable, rectangular surf mat consisting of four pontoons stuck together.

It is suitable for beginners, so children start learning surfing with it.

(v) **Body Surfing** In this, the wave is surfed without a board, using the surfer's own body to catch and ride the wave. It is considered by some to be the purest form of surfing, but it is the most difficult, requiring much practice.

5. Explain how paragliding is carried out. Suggest three precautions to be followed before and while engaging in this sport.

Ans. The paraglider is a lightweight, free flying, foot-launched glider aircraft with no rigid primary structure.

Paragliding is carried out with the pilot sitting in harness suspended below a fabric wing comprising a large number of interconnected cells.

Three precautions to be followed before and while engaging in paragliding are as follows

(i) **Knowledge, Ability and Mental Strength** It is advisable to practise for endurance and physical strength, as these will have great impact on your success.

A quicker way to enhance your ability is to take your glider to a field and tirelessly work on your ground handling.

Knowledge is gained by searching websites, reading blogs and books, through which one can have knowledge about the basics, flying, weather and also about performing first aid.

(ii) **Favourable Weather** It is the most important constraint to manage even for people with a high level of experience.

It is always important to watch the forecast from a reliable source before leaving for paragliding.

Wind is the main factor, whereby strong and straight wind can turn out to be very disastrous.

(iii) **Good Landing Site** Visibility and accessibility are some of the factors that should be considered when looking for a good paragliding site. Irregular and rough landings may lead to fractured bones.

It is also advisable to go for paragliding spots with visible wind indicators to assist you on which direction to take.

• Case Based Questions

1. Students of Doon Public School are going for the adventure sports 'Trekking'. You are the team leader and incharge of all the students. You have told the students about the safety measures that they should follow during trekking. In your group, there are 20 boys in the age group of 14 to 16 years.

Based on this case, answer the following questions.

(i) Which type of trekking will you choose for your students?

Ans. As a team leader, I will choose easy trekking as the school students are the beginners. Easy trekking includes easy climbing to hills of low elevation.

(ii) What things should be carried while going for trekking?

Ans. Food, water, bedding, tent, clothes, stove, cooking kit and medical kit should be carried for trekking.

2. Ravi is a trainer for the adventure sport river rafting. He often takes river rafting activities on the mountain rivers. A group of 5 boys aged between 15-18 years asked him to train them.

Based on this case, answer the following questions

(i) Which grade should be chosen by Ravi to train those boys?

Ans. Grade I or II should be chosen by Ravi as the river has small waves, almost flat water and free or very little obstacles. These grades are done by beginners.

(ii) If one of the boys do not know swimming, should Ravi train him?

Ans. It is not advisable as having adequate capabilities of swimming is a safety measure during river rafting.

3. Sports is one of the most effective physical activities that provide innumerable health benefits. Ensuring safety in sports is essential to prevent any sports injuries. It is important that we take care of our body in performing sports and even fitness related activities.

(i) What are the protective gears that a person should wear in paragliding?

Ans. In paragliding, the helmet, mouth guards, gloves, protective pads and proper shoes are essential to wear.

(ii) How adventure sports is different from sports?

Ans. Adventure sports involve outdoor sports that have high level of risks or danger. Sports are the forms of organised activities that are played for recreation and do not involve risks or danger.

Chapter Test

Multiple Choice Questions

1. The board whose length is less than 7 feet is called
    (a) Long board   (b) Mat board
    (c) Knee board   (d) Short board

2. The leaders of physical education has both _______ and _______ qualities.
    (a) Acquired   (b) Innate
    (c) Both (a) and (b)   (d) None of these

3. Choose the incorrect option
    (a) A good leader executes the plans well   (b) Mountain biking is an example of mountain sports
    (c) Rock climbing is also done on artificial walls   (d) Trekking is also known as backpaking

4. Find the odd one out
    (a) Surfing   (b) Skating
    (c) Mountaineering   (d) Skiing

5. In this grade, the river has huge waves. The level is tough and thus rafting requires great physical endurance and mental toughness. People may also face severe injuries or even death.

Which grade of river rafting is being talked about?
    (a) Grade II   (b) Grade I
    (c) Grade IV   (d) Grade VI

Short Answer (SA) Type Questions

6. Why is it essential to wear protective gears in adventure sports?

7. List three ways of preventing injuries in paragliding.

8. Write a short note on the adventure activity of trekking.

9. Why mountaineering is so popular as an adventure activity?

10. Mention three qualities developed by participating in adventure sports.

Long Answer (LA) Type Questions

11. Explain the different grades of river rafting.

12. What safety precautions or measures should be taken to prevent any sport injury?

Answers

1. (d)   *2.* (c)   *3.* (b)   *4.* (a)   *5.* (d)

CHAPTER 04

Psychology and Sports

In this Chapter...

- Meaning and Definition of Psychology
- Growth and Development
- Adolescent Problems and their Management

A sport or a physical activity is essentially a mind game. It is a place where a small difference in mental powers often makes a big difference between success and failure. Thus, there came to be an understanding of importance of the inter-relatedness of sports and psychology.

In simple words, in physical education and sports, it is very important to understand the psychological aspects of an individual or sportsperson.

Meaning and Definition of Psychology

The word 'psychology' is derived from a Greek word 'Psyche' meaning 'soul' and 'logos' meaning 'scientific study'. Hence, psychology came to be understood as the scientific study of the soul. However, this definition of psychology was discarded and psychology was defined as 'science of mind'.

With time and further research, the definition of psychology kept on changing. It became the 'science of consciousness' and finally reached to its most accepted and latest definition as the, 'science of human behaviour'.

Various psychologists and scientists defined psychology in different ways.

Some accepted definitions of psychology are

- According to **WB Pillsbury and JB Watson**, "Psychology is the science of human behaviour."

- According to **Woodworth**, "Psychology deals with the activities of the individual in relation to his environment."
- According to the **Oxford Dictionary**, "Psychology is the scientific study of human mind and its functions, especially those affecting behaviour in a given context."
- According to **Crow and Crow**, "Psychology is the study of human behaviour and human relationships."

Meaning and Definition of Sports Psychology

The increasing importance of the field of psychology in sports and physical education lead to the emergence of a new discipline called Sports Psychology.

Sports psychology is the branch of applied psychology that deals with the performance and behaviour of an individual while performing sports and any other physical activity.

It is a multidisciplinary science that uses psychological knowledge and skills to address optimal performance and well-being of athletes, developmental and social aspects of sports participation, and systemic issues associated with sports settings and organisations.

In other words, sports psychology involves the study of how psychological factors, such as behaviour, arousal, motivation and aspiration, affect performance and how participation in sports and exercise affect psychological and physical factors.

Various eminent psychologists asserted such an understanding of sports psychology in different terms. Some of them are as follows

- According to **RN Singer**, "Sports psychology is encompassing scholarly educational and practical activities associated with the understanding and influencing of selected behaviours of people in athletics, physical education, vigorous recreational activity and exercise."
- According to **Clark and Clark**, "Sports psychology is an applied psychology. It is more concerned with the personalities, emotional or motivational aspects of sports and physical activities. It employs many of the techniques used in psychology."
- According to **John Lauther**, "Sports psychology is an area which attempts to apply psychological facts and principles to learning performance and associated human behaviour in whole field of sports."
- According to **KM Burns**, "Sports psychology for physical education is that branch of psychology which deals with the physical fitness of an individual through his participation in games and sports."

Importance of Psychology in Physical Education and Sports

In the present scenario, sports psychology is becoming increasingly important, particularly with respect to the improvement and maintenance of athletic performance.

With its purpose being the modification of behaviour according to the needs of a situation, sports psychology helps to improve attitudes and mental skills to help sportspersons perform well.

It helps to identify limited beliefs, behaviours and attitudes that act as obstacles in good performance and helps to embrace a healthier philosophy during performance.

Sports psychology also helps the coaches to make a good coaching technique that conditions and prepares a player to deal with stress situations while being mentally ready and confident.

The following points highlight the importance of sports psychology

1. **Enhancement of Physiological Capacities** Sports psychology plays a unique role in the enhancement of physiological capacities such as strength, speed, flexibility etc. Motivation and proper feedback plays a major role in the enhancement of physical capacity of sportspersons. It is an established fact that psychological capacity or power can increase physiological capacities of individuals.

2. **Learning Motor Skills** Sports psychology plays a major role in learning motor skills. Such a learning depends on the individual's level of readiness, *i.e.* both physiological and psychological readiness.

   Physiological readiness in children is the development of necessary strength, flexibility and endurance, while psychological readiness is related to the learner's state of mind, *i.e.* the desire and willingness to learn the particular skill.

   Sports psychology plays an essential part in understanding psychological readiness and interests as well as attitudes of an individual towards efficient learning and performance of a motor skill.

3. **Understanding Behaviour** Sports psychology helps in understanding the behaviour of athletes or sportspersons engaged in competitive sports.

   Coaches also come to know the interest, attitude towards a physical activity, instinct, drive and personality of a sportsperson.

4. **Controlling Emotions** Sports psychology plays an important role in controlling the emotions of sportspersons during practice as well as in competition.

   Spontaneous and uncontrolled outbursts of emotions such as anger, fear, negative self thinking, etc., may lead to a decline in performance. Hence, it is essential to control emotions during sports competitions.

   Sports psychology plays a vital role at such a juncture, as it helps in balancing the arousal of emotions, which further improves performance.

5. **Psychological Preparation for Competition** Sports psychology plays a significant role in the psychological preparation of an athlete.

   It focuses on improving mental abilities such as concentration, confidence, etc. reducing stress, and building the competitive spirit among the athletes. Owing to this feature, today, sports psychologist services are required for many national and international level games.

6. **Helps Solve Emotional Problems of Sportspersons** Stress, tension and anxiety are natural during competitions or tournaments as well as during practice/training.

   There may be some other emotional problems such as depression, frustration, anorexia, panic, etc. Knowledge of sports psychology is helpful in such situations. Techniques of relaxation and concentration for stress management can be applied by sportspersons who are facing such problems.

Thus, it can be said that sports psychology plays a vital role in enhancing the performance of sportspersons. It deals with various mental qualities such as concentration, confidence, emotional control, commitment, etc., which are important for successful performance in sports and games.

Growth and Development

It is an accepted fact that physical education aims at the holistic development of an individual. All physical activities and sports are very essential for proper growth and development of a child.

Thus, the knowledge of growth and development is essential for physical education teachers as well as parents.

Without sufficient knowledge of the process of growth and development of humans, it is impossible to understand the physical, mental, social and emotional development of their students/children.

Generally, growth and development are used as synonyms. However, the definitions of these terms indicate a very minute difference between them.

Meaning and Definition of Growth

The word 'growth' implies an increase in size. It is the physical change that an individual goes through certain stages in life. Whenever a person undergoes growth, it essentially means that his/her organs or body parts have become larger and heavier. It is thus an increase in size, height, weight and length of a human body.

Various definitions of growth given by scholars are

- According to **Hurlock**, "Growth is change in size, in proportion, disappearance of old features and acquisition of new ones."

- According to **Crow and Crow**, "Growth refers to structural and physiological changes."

Meaning and Definition of Development

The term 'development' is referred to as an improvement in functioning. It refers to the continuous process of qualitative changes in the organism as whole which leads to maturity.

In other words, it is a process by which physical, emotional and intellectual changes occur so as to improve the working and functioning of the body. Various definitions of development given by scholars include

- According to **EB Herlock**, "Development means a progressive series of changes that occur in an orderly predictable pattern as a result of maturation and experience."

- According to **Gesell**, "Development can be observed and to a certain extent, measured and evaluated. Its evaluation and measurement can be done in three ways, *i.e.* anatomical, physiological and behavioural."

Differences between Growth and Development

From the above given definitions of growth and development, one can say that development is more wider and comprehensive term than growth.

The differences between growth and development are summarised in the table given below

Growth	Development
It refers to the physical changes in the height, weight, shape and size of an individual.	It refers to the overall cognitive changes in the shape, form and structures that result in improved functioning.
It is one aspect of development. It may or may not bring development.	It is a more comprehensive term that includes growth. It is possible without growth.
It is quantitative and thus can be measured.	It is qualitative and thus cannot be measured. It can only be observed.
It is not a continuous step. It stops at a particular age of physical maturity.	It is a life-long process.
It is based on biological parameters that grow externally (physically) and naturally.	It includes psychological, social as well as mental growth. They are internal and are emphasised by individual behavioural factors.
It is related to one aspect of personality.	It looks at personality as a whole.

Both growth and development differ in definition, but in a wider and a practical sense both the terms are used collectively.

Both of them refer to the changes in physical, intellectual, social, and emotional aspects of human life. Thus, growth and development go hand in hand.

This is a stage of complex changes which brings us to the stage that will end the childhood and lead to adulthood.

- This stage marks the start of puberty i.e. a series of complex physical changes that marks the beginning of sexual maturity.

  It brings remarkable change in the shape of an individual such as breast development, muscular changes, bone hardening, change in voice, pimples, etc.

Adolescent Problems and their Management

Adolescence

Spanning between 13 to 19 years, adolescence is a stage, when the individual becomes integrated with the society of adults by undergoing marked intellectual and sexual transformations.

Adolescence is a very important stage of development as it faces rapid and important physical developments.

The term 'Adolescence' is derived from a Latin word 'Adolescere' meaning 'to grow to maturity'. It is a period which fills the gap between childhood and adulthood.

According to **Stanley Hall**, "Adolescence is a period of great stress and strain, storm and strife." In fact, it is a period of growth and development that acts as a bridge of transition from childhood to adulthood.

According to **Jersield**, "Adolescence is that span of years during which boys and girls move from childhood to adulthood mentally, emotionally, socially and physically."

This stage has been identified as a period of storm and stress. The adolescent undergoes extreme variations in emotions.

In a state of instability, as they are not sure of their capacities, interests and the treatment, they face intense emotions, confusion and rebellion nature between being independent and dependent in different situations.

Therefore, the lack of balance and understanding in the changes happening in their lives results in lot of problems that the adolescents face in their day-to-day lives.

Thus, the knowledge of these problems and how to manage them becomes crucial not only for educators but for parents as well. With this knowledge, they can help the children in laying a strong foundation for them and teach them to solve such problems for the future.

Problems Faced by Adolescents

Due to the sudden and rapid biological, psychological and behavioural changes taking place in the body, an adolescent suffers through many problems.

The only source of comfort during these times, for them, are their peers with whom they might develop bad habits. Hence, it is essential to know these problems as well as the bad habits that an adolescent may develop.

The problems of adolescents are described as follows

1. **Physical and Biological Problems** In the stage of adolescence, both girls and boys go through immense bodily changes. Girls start menstruating and nightfall starts in boys. The lack of knowledge of such changes makes the adolescents feel restless and worried.
   As a result, they often go through the sleepless nights and are unable to rest leading to various health problems.

2. **Issues of Stability and Adjustment** Adolescents becomes highly conscious of themself and of the world around them.
   They try to find themselfs a place within this world.
   However, adolescents constantly go through the changes which makes them unstable.

Their behaviour become erratic as they are not able to adjust themselves to such changes.

Therefore, they find it difficult to coordinate and adjust easily with others. They feel that they are constantly under pressure and desire a free atmosphere.

3. **Aggression and Uncontrollable Emotions** Adolescents are very emotional and hyper. They go through sudden change of mood and outbursts almost every day.
   One aspect of this suddenness of change include the thoughts of suicide, self-hate, anxiety and depression that they may face.
   Adolescents also display aggressive behaviour. They overreact to minor situations and are rebellious towards criticism. This may get them into bad anti-social habits and also may land them into problems that may affect their future.

4. **Social Standing** Adolescents are very conscious of their social status and their personal identity. They want to make their own respectable place in the society while fitting into it. To fit perfectly, they come under peer pressure which sometimes leads them into wrong means of obtaining luxurious things.
   They feel themselves to be important and demand the same respect from others. They sometimes become overconfident and try to hide their mistakes. They put their blame on others and protect themselves.

5. **Problems Related to Sex** In contrast to the previous stages, adolescents now are more attracted to the opposite sex. Their urges related to this attraction is so strong that they become restless and may take wrong means to attain them.

6. **Mental Problems** At this stage, children suffer from immense stress, anxiety and tension. With a lot of things going on around them, their emotions are uncontrollable and their concentration power declines. This severely affects their studies and also results in many social problems.

7. **Drug Addiction** The imbalance and instability that the adolescents face lead them towards developing bad habits. In addition, the curiosity, lack of knowledge and peer pressure leads them towards the drugs and alcohol. This experimentation can turn into addiction which can spoil the entire future of the teenager.

8. **Criminal Activities** The desire to be accepted by the peers and the restlessness, as a result of changes occurring in their lives, makes them more inclined to participate in criminal activities. Adolescents indulge in criminal offences like thefts, stealing, violence, molestation, etc.

Management of Adolescent Problems

The problems of adolescence should be managed and addressed promptly, otherwise it may spoil the life of the adolescents. They may be the victims of smoking, drug abuse, alcohol, unsafe abortions (girls) and other undesirable activities.

The following techniques may be used for the management of adolescent problems

1. **Proper Counselling** The problems of adolescence are the result of natural growth and development of the body. At this time, lack of experience develops shyness, introversion etc. in them. It prevents them from expressing their problems to their elders.

   This condition may increase their mental tension. Therefore, proper counselling and guidance by parents, teachers and elders is the best method for the management of adolescent problems.

2. **Participation in Co-curricular Activities** Adolescence is an age of energy and dynamism. If the energy is utilised in activities other than academics *i.e.* sports, dance, social functions etc, their surplus energy is spent properly. As a result, emotional upheavals as well as instability will not occur.

   This helps in the development of their motor skills and in harmonising the personality of an adolescent.

3. **Mutual Understanding** Family members and all elders must try to understand the problems of adolescents. They should be symphathetic and affectionate towards them and must try to build a relationship with them.

   At the same time, adolescents must also understand that their parents are trying to help them for their betterment. With such a mutual understanding, teenagers feeling of instability can reduce and they may not get stressed and anxious.

4. **Recognition of Individuality** Adolescents are often disturbed by being treated as a small child. So, parents must recognise the opinions and views of such teenagers.

   They need respect and responsibility just like every other adult. Hence, parents must not constantly correct them and scold them.

5. **Sex Education** Adolescents must be educated about sex, just like any other lessons taught in school, in a straightforward way. Correct knowledge enables them to understand the changes occurring in the their body as well as their urges better.

   They must be properly guided to tackle all the problems related to sex as well as to channelise their drives towards constructive work.

6. **Religious and Moral Education** Religious and moral education is very important for managing adolescents.

   It will give them mental peace and some problems like indiscipline, anxiety and worry will be sorted out easily.

7. **Suitable Environment** Adolescents should be provided suitable environment for growth and development. They should be taught how to behave and live.

   Parents must look after the health and diet of adolescents and provide them a safe and healthy environment for growth and development.

8. **Adequate Independence** Adolescents value freedom and independence. They want to express their views and feelings independently.

   They desire to take their own decision and are irritated when any order or restriction is imposed on them. Hence, parents must give them adequate freedom and try to understand their sentiments.

   Therefore, it can be observed that adolescence is the age of struggle. It is very necessary to give proper attention to them, so that they are able to manage their problems during this crucial phase of growth and development.

Chapter Practice

Objective Questions

• Multiple Choice Questions

1. According to its Greek meaning, psychology came to be understood as
(a) Scientific study of soul   (b) Study of behaviour
(c) Study of mind   (d) Study of consciousness
Ans. (a) According to its Greek meaning, psychology came to be understood as Scientific study of soul.

2. According to whome, 'Psychology is the science of human behaviour?
(a) WB Pillsbury   (b) JB Watson
(c) Both (a) and (b)   (d) None of these
Ans. (c) According to WB Pillsbury and JB Watson, 'Psychology is the science of human behaviour'.

3. The term _______ is referred to as an improvement in functioning.
(a) Growth   (b) Development
(c) Phycology   (d) Adolescent
Ans. (b) The term development is referred to as an improvement in functioning.

4. According to whom 'Development can be observed and to a certain extent measures and evaluated. Its revaluation and measurement can be done in three ways, i.e., anatomical, physiological and behavioural'?
(a) Crow and Crow   (b) Gesell
(c) Herlock   (d) Woodwroth
Ans. (b) According to Gesell 'Development can be observed upto some extent, measures and evaluated. Its revaluation and measurement can be done in three ways, i.e., anatomical, physiological and behavioural'.

5. Growth is considered which type of process?
(a) Continuous process   (b) Quantitative process
(c) Qualitative process   (d) Both (a) and (b)
Ans. (b) Growth is considered as a quantitative process as it can be measured.

6. Pinky is a 13 year old girl. She has an elder sister of 19 years and a younger brother of 5 years. Pinky falls in the age group of
(a) Infants   (b) Childhood
(c) Adolescents   (d) Adulthood
Ans. (c) Pinky falls in the age group of adolescent. This stage spans from 13 to 19 years.

7. Which of the following is a problem faced by adolescents?
(a) Drug addiction   (b) Social standing
(c) Aggression   (d) All of these
Ans. (d) Problems faced by adolescents are drug addiction, social standing, aggression, etc.

8. Ajay is the coach of a Basketball team. He often notices that the team members do not play as a team. They are more interested in playing individually. What kind of issues the members are having?
(a) Behaviourial issues   (b) Emotional problems
(c) Problems in motor skills   (d) All of these
Ans. (a) The team members are going through behavioural issues as they are not playing as a single unit but are more interested in their individual performances.

9. Atul noticed that his 14 year old son has become very emotional and hyper. He overeacts in minor situations and becomes too protective of himself. What problems is he going through?
(a) Physical problems   (b) Uncontrollable emotions
(c) Both (a) and (b)   (d) Neither (a) nor (b)
Ans. (b) Atul's 14 year old son is facing the problem of uncontrollable emotions as he becomes very emotional and hyper. He is going through the stage of adolescence. Children in this stage go through sudden change of mood and outbursts.

10. Match the following.

	List I		List II
A.	Mental problems	1.	Height, weight
B.	Physical changes	2.	Self hate, depression
C.	Unstable emotions	3.	Stress, tension, anxiety
D.	Social standing	4.	Confusion, personal identity

Codes

	A	B	C	D			A	B	C	D
(a)	1	4	2	3		(b)	3	1	2	4
(c)	2	3	4	1		(d)	3	4	1	2

Ans. (b) The correct match is A-3, B-1, C-2, D-4.

11. Amans parents feel that Aman is acquiring some bad habits like lying, stealing and even fighting with his peers. He should be taken to a ________.

(a) Physician   (b) Physical education instruction

(c) Counsellor   (d) Sports academy

Ans. (c) Aman should be taken to a counsellor so that the counsellor can talk to Aman and understand the feelings and emotions that he is going through.

• Assertion-Reasoning MCQs

Directions (Q. Nos. 1-4) *Each of these questions contains two statements, Assertion (A) and Reason (R). Each of these questions also has four alternative choices, any one of which is the correct answer. You have to select one of the codes (a), (b), (c) and (d) given below.*

Codes

(a) Both A and R are true and R is the correct explanation of A

(b) Both A and R are true, but R is not the correct explanation of A

(c) A is true, but R is false

(d) A is false, but R is true

1. **Assertion** (A) Psychology is the science of human behaviour.

Reason (R) Psychology is not related to sports.

Ans. (c) The Assertion is true as the subject of psychology deals with the thinking pattern of human mind that influences human behaviour.

The Reason is false as psychology influences the behaviour and thinking of a sports person so it is related to sports also. Thus, Assertion A is true, but R is false.

2. **Assertion** (A) Sports psychology plays a major role in learning motor skills.

Reason (R) Growth refers to structural and physiological changes.

Ans. (b) The assertion is true as sports psychology influences the learning capabilities of the players and enables them to grasp specific motor skills needed in sports. Reason is also true as growth changes the physical structure of human being. It also brings Psychological changes. But reason do not explains assertion. Thus, both A and R are true and R is not the correct explanation of A.

3. **Assertion** (A) Growth is qualitative in nature.

Reason (R) Adolescents face many problems including the problem of social standing.

Ans. (d) The concept of growth is quantative in nature, it is not qualitative. Adolescent is the age group that faces lot of problems due to their social standing. They are confused about themselves, their needs and their abilities. Thus, A is false but R is true.

4. **Assertion** (A) Adolescent age period is quite dynamic in nature.

Reason (R) In this age group, both girls and boys go through the emotional and physical changes.

Ans. (a) Assertion is true as the age group of adolescents undergo extreme variations emotional variations, interests, capacities and physical changes.

Reason is also true as adolescent boys and girls go through lot of changes physically and emotionally. Reason correctly explains assertion. Thus, Both A and R are correct and R is the correct explanation of A.

• Case Based MCQs

1. Sports psychology is important for coaches also, to understand the behaviour patterns of sports persons in different situations and to modify their behaviours accordingly. The coaches then are able to understand various emotions faced by the sports persons like fear, anger, disgust, aggression, frustration etc.

(i) Sports psychology is helpful for which of the following?

(a) Sports coaches

(b) Sports persons

(c) Physical eduction teachess

(d) All of above these

Ans. (d) Sports psychology is a subject that is helpful in understanding the behaviour of sports persons, so it is helpful for coaches, physical education teachers and sports persons.

(ii) Sports psychology plays a significant role in ______.

(a) Understanding behaviours

(b) Solving emotional problems

(c) Both (a) and (b)

(d) None of the above

Ans. (c) Sports psychology plays a significant role in both i.e. understanding behaviours of the sport spersons as well as in solving their emotional problems.

(iii) With the help of sports psychology, coaches can better understand which of the following?

(a) Growth

(b) Development

(c) Aggression

(d) Physical Education

Ans. (c) With the help of sports psychology, coaches can better understand the aggression in sports person. They can then look for the causes and ways of treating them.

2. Mohit is a 17-year-old football player. When he was the captain of the football team, then he played really well. But from the past 3 months, his performance is deteriorated. He is specially showing his aggression to David, who is now the captain of football team.

Based on this case answer the following question

(i) Why Mohit's performance is going down?
   (a) Due to physical problems
   (b) Uncontrollable emotions
   (c) Lack of balance
   (d) Adjustment issues

Ans. (b) Mohit's performance is going down due to uncontrollable emotions. He is getting very emotional and hyper. He is constantly under pressure.

(ii) The cause of Mohits aggressive behaviour towards David is
   (a) David's popularity
   (b) Mohit's captaincy
   (c) David's captaincy
   (d) None of the above

Ans. (c) Cause of Mohit's aggressive behaviour towards David is his captaincy. Earlier, he was the captain of the team. Now when David is the captain, Mohit is not able to adjust with the situation and feels bad.

(iii) Mohit is in which age group?
   (a) Adoloscent   (b) Adulthood
   (c) Childhood   (d) Infant

Ans. (a) Mohit is in the age group of adolescent. This age group spans between 13 to 19 years.

PART 2
Subjective Questions

• Short Answer Type Questions

1. Write a short note on sports psychology.

Ans. Sports psychology is the branch of applied psychology that deals with the performance and behaviour of individual while performing sports and any other physical activity. It is multidisciplinary science that uses psychological knowledge and skills to address optimal performance and well-being of athletes, developmental and social aspects of sports participation and systemic issues associated with sports settings and organisations.

In other words, sports psychology involves the study of how psychological factors, such as behaviour, arousal, motivation and aspiration, affect performance and how participation in sport and exercise affect psychological and physical factors.

2. How sports psychology helps in learning motor skills?

Ans. Sports psychology plays a major role in learning motor skills. It helps in identifying the behaviour and attitudes of players. This knowledge can then be applied to develop strength, speed, endurance, flexibility, etc.

Sports psychology plays an essential part in understanding psychological readiness and interests of an individual towards learning a particular skill. Accordingly, that skill can be developed by enhancing the motor skills needed to develop a particular area.

It helps coaches to design a good coaching technique that conditions and prepares players to use particular motor skills.

3. Explain the concept of growth.

Ans. The word 'growth' implies an increase in size. It is the physical change that an individual goes through certain stages in life. Whenever a person undergoes growth, it essentially means that his/her organs or body parts have become larger and heavier. It is thus an increase in size, height, weight and length of a human body.

Various definitions of growth given by scholars are as follows

• According to Hurlock, "Growth is change in size, in proportion, disappearance of old features and acquisition of new ones."

• According to Crow and Crow, "Growth refers to structural and physiological changes".

4. What is development, explain with the help of definitions.

Ans. The term 'development' is referred to an improvement in functioning. It refers to the continuous process of qualitative changes in the organism as whole which leads to maturity.

In other words, it is a process by which physical, emotional and intellectual changes occur so as to improve the working and functioning of the body.

Various definitions of development given by scholars include

• According to EB Herlock, "Development means a progressive series of changes that occur in an orderly predictable pattern as a result of maturation and experience."

• According to Gesell, "Development can be observed and to a certain extent, measured and evaluated. Its evaluation and measurement can be done in three ways, i.e. anatomical, physiological and behavioural."

5. Why adolescence is identified as a period of storm and stress?

Ans. Adolescence is identified as a period of storm and stress as in this stage boys and girls face extreme variations in their emotions. They go through a state of instability.

In a state of instability, they are not sure of their capacities, interests they face intense emotions, confusion and rebellion nature between being independent and dependent in different situations.

The lack of balance and understanding in the changes happening in their lives results in lot of problems that the adolescents face in their day-to-day lives. Therefore, this period is also called as period of storm and stress.

6. List three problems faced by adolescents.

Ans. Three problems faced by adolescents are as under

Aggression Adolescents display aggressive behaviour. They overreact to minor situations and are rebellious towards criticism. This may get them into bad anti-social habits and also may land them into problems that may affect their future.

Drug Addition The imbalance and instability that the adolescents face lead them towards developing bad habits. In addition, the curiosity, lack of knowledge and peer pressure lead them towards the drugs and alcohol. This experiementation can turn into addiction which can spoil the entire future of the teenager.

Criminal Activities The desire to be accepted by the peers and the restlessness, as a result of changes occurring in their lives, makes them more inclined to participate in criminal activities. Adolescents indulge in criminal offences like thefts, stealing, violence, molestation, etc.

7. Explain the physical, mental and adjustment problems of adolescents.

Ans. The physical, mental and adjustment problems of adolescents are explained as follows

(i) **Physical problems** In the stage of adolescence, both girls and boys go through immense bodily changes. Girls start menstruating and nightfall starts in boys. The lack of knowledge of such changes makes the adolescents feel restless and worried.

As a result, they often go through sleepless nights and are unable to rest, leading to various health problems.

(ii) **Mental Problems** At this stage, children suffer from immense stress, anxiety and tension. With a lot of things going on around them, their emotions are uncontrollable and their concentration power declines. This severely affects their studies and also results in many social problems.

(iii) **Issues of Adjustment** An adolescent becomes highly conscious of himself/herself and of the world around him/her. He/She tries to find for himself/herself a place within this world. Adolescents are confused about their identity so they face various adjustment problems.

8. What are the techniques used for the management of adolescent problems? Explain any two?

Ans. Techniques used for the management of adolescent problems are as follows

(i) Proper Counselling

(ii) Participation in Co-curricular Activities

(iii) Mutual Understanding

(iv) Recognition of Individuality

(v) Sex Education

(vi) Religious and Moral Education

(vii) Suitable Environment

(viii) Adequate Independence

Mutual Understanding Family members and all elders must try to understand the problems of adolescents. They should be symphathetic and affectionate towards them and must try to build a relationship with them.

Recognition of Individuality Adolescents are often disturbed by being treated as a small child. So, parents must recognise the opinions and views of such teenagers.

9. In what way a counsellor can help an adolescent if he/she faces emotional problems?

Ans. It is important to manage the problems of adolescence. Otherwise it will become a hindrance in the normal growth and development of a teenager. A counsellor can help an adolescent in facing emotional problems by the following ways

- A counsellor can hear their problems and provide them guidance.

- They can solve the emotional problems in a better way as they are trained.

- They can suggest ways to control aggression, frustration, anxiety, etc. It leads to their proper growth and development.

- Adolescent children can also talk openly and freely to a counsellor and discuss about the ways of coping up.

• Long Answer (LA) Type Questions

1. How is psychology important for sports persons?

Ans. Sports psychology plays a very important role in improving the performance of a sportsperson. Its importance is clearly highlighted below

(i) **Enhancement of Physiological Capacities** Sports psychology plays a unique role in the enhancement of physiological capacities such as strength, speed, flexibility etc.

Motivation and proper feedback plays a major role in the enhancement of physical capacity of a sportsperson.

(ii) **Learning Motor Skills** Sports psychology plays a major role in learning motor skills, such as learning depends on the individual's level of readiness, i.e. both physiological and psychological readiness.

It plays an essential role towards an individual attitudes understanding psychological readiness and interests in efficient learning and performance of a motor skill.

(iii) **Psychological Preparation for Competition** Sports psychology plays a significant role in the psychological preparation of an athlete. It focuses on improving mental abilities, reducing stress, and building the competitive spirit among athletes.

(iv) **Understanding Behaviour** Sports psychology helps in understanding the behaviour of athletes or sports persons engaged in competitive sports.

Coaches also come to know the interest, attitude towards physical activity, instinct, drive and personality of a sportsperson.

(v) **Controlling Emotions** Sports psychology plays an important role in controlling the emotions of sportspersons during practice as well as in competition.

Spontaneous and uncontrollable outbursts of emotions such as anger, fear etc. may lead to decline in performance. Hence, it is important to control emotions during competitions.

Sports psychology plays a vital role at such a juncture, as it helps in balancing the arousal of emotions, which further improves performance.

(vi) **Helps to Solve Emotional Problems of Sportspersons** Stress, tension and anxiety are natural during competitions or tournaments as well as during practice/training.

There may be some other emotional problems such as depression, frustration, anorexia, panic, etc. Knowledge of sports psychology is helpful in such situations.

Techniques of relaxation and concentration for stress management can be applied by sportspersons who are facing such problems.

2. Mention six differences between growth and development.

Ans. Differences between growth and development are as follows

Growth	Development
It refers to the physical changes in the height, weight, shape and size of an individual.	It refers to the overall cognitive changes in the shape, form and structures that result in improved functioning.
It is one aspect of development. It may or may not bring development.	It is more comprehensive term that includes growth. It is possible without growth.
It is quantitative and thus can be measured.	It is qualitative and thus cannot be measured. It can only be observed.
It is not a continuous step. It stops at a particular age of physical maturity.	It is a life-long process.
It is based on biological parameters that grow externally (physically) and naturally.	In includes psychological, social as well as mental growth. They are internal and are emphasised by individual behavioural factors.
It is related to one aspect of personality.	It looks at personality as a whole.

3. Discuss five problems faced by adolescents.

Ans. The problems faced by adolescents are as follows

(i) **Aggression and Uncontrollable Emotions** Adolescents are very emotional and hyper. They go through sudden change of mood and outbursts almost every day. One aspect of this suddenness of change include the thoughts of suicide, self-hate, anxiety and depression that they may face.

Adolescents also display aggressive behaviour. They overreact to minor situations and rebellious towards criticism. This may get them into bad anti-social habits and also may land them into problems that may affect their future.

(ii) **Social Standing** Adolescents are very conscious of their social status and their personal identity. They want to make their own respectable place in the society while fitting into it. To fit perfectly, they come under peer pressure which sometimes leads them into wrong means of obtaining luxurious things.

They feel themselves to be improtant and demand the same respect from others. They sometimes become overconfident and try to hide their mistakes. They put their blame on others and protect themselves.

(iii) **Problems Related to Sex** In contrast to the previous stages, adolescents now are more attracted to the opposite sex. Their urges related to this attraction is so strong that they become restless and may take wrong means to attain them.

(iv) **Drug Addiction** The imbalance and instability that the adolescents face lead them towards developing bad habits. In addition, the curiosity, lack of knowledge and peer pressure leads them towards the drugs and alcohol. This experimentation can turn into addiction which can spoil the entire future of the teenager.

(v) **Criminal Activities** The desire to be accepted by the peers and the restlessness as a result of changes occurring in their lives, makes them more inclined to participate in criminal activities. Adolescents indulge in criminal offences like thefts, stealing, violence, molestation, etc.

• Case Based Questions

1. Praveen is in his adolescence and he lives in society 'Y'. During a councelling session in his school he informs councellor about his bad habits of stealing, drug dealing, etc. Praveen knows that stealing is a crime and he wants to get rid of this bad habit. He is also aware that drug dealing is an offence and morally wrong.

Based on this case, answer the following questions.

(i) How environment can hamper Praveen's behaviour?

Ans. Adolescents acquire the habits and behaviour that they see around them so if Praveen lives in an environment where there are criminal activities taking place, then he will acquire those.

(ii) How a suitable environment can be given to Praveen?

Ans. Praveen's parents must look after him and teach him how to behave and live. They should guide him and provide him a safe and healthy environment.

2. Ruchi is a student of class 9 and is new to the school hostel. Her warden is worried as she is not taking her meals and wants to leave the hostel and go home. She is not taking interest in any kind of school activities either. She do not interacts with other students also.

Based on this, answer the following questions

(i) Why Ruchi wants to go home?

Ans. Ruchi wants to go home because she is not able to adjust herself to the hostel life. She is finding difficulty in coordinating and is constantly under pressure.

(ii) In which age group is Ruchi? Why is she facing problems?

Ans. Ruchi is in the age group of adolescence. In this stage, adolescents become highly conscious of themselves, their behaviour become erratic and their emotions are unstable.

3. The knowledge of growth and development is essential for physical education teachers as well as parents. Without sufficient knowledge of the process of growth and development in humans, it is impossible to understand the physical, mental, social and emotional development of their students/Children.

Based on the passage, answer the following questions.

(i) Why development is called a life long process?

Ans. Development is considered as a life long process as it is continuous and do not stops at a particular age of physical or mental maturity.

(ii) What is the major difference between growth and development, in the context of psychology?

Ans. Growth is defined as the physical change that a particular individual undergoes during certain stages in his lifetime, whereas development is the overall change of the individual in terms of his physique, behaviour, emotions and cognition throughout his lifespan.

Multiple Choice Questions

1. The term '______' is referred to as an improvement in functioning.
   (a) Development
   (b) Growth
   (c) Both (a) and (b)
   (d) None of these

2. Identify the incorrect statement
   (a) Growth pattern is different for everyone
   (b) Adolescents may become victim of criminal activities
   (c) Adolescents face physical instability
   (d) Cognitive ability is part of development

3. A new discipline that merges psychology and physical activity and games is
   (a) Applied psychology
   (b) Sports psychology
   (c) Both (a) and (b)
   (d) None of these

4. ______ means a progressive series of changes that occur in an orderly pattern
   (a) Growth
   (b) Psychology
   (c) Behaviour
   (d) Development.

5. Growth and development are never ending process.

   It starts from the period when a person is not born and continues upto death. These changes are constantly taking place related to physical and psychological abilities and capacities. Growth and development are often used to describe these changes. Based on the passage answer the following questions

   What is the meaning of development?
   (a) Change in structure of body organ
   (b) Change in size
   (c) Change in maturity
   (d) All of these

Short Answer (SA) Type Questions

1. How mutual understanding between parents/ teacher and adolescents help in knowing them better?

2. How sports can help in solving emotional problems of the adolescents?

Long Answer (LA) Type Question

1. What advice should be given to teachers and parents to solve the problems of adolescent children?

2. Explain any three techniques for management of adolescent problems?

Answers

1. (a)   *2.* (c)   *3.* (b)   *4.* (d)   *5.* (d)

CHAPTER 05

Training and Doping in Sports

In this Chapter...

- Meaning and Definition of Sports Training
- Principles of Sports Training
- Concept of Doping
- Prohibited Substances and Methods

Today, sports and physical education are specialised fields. All sports and physical activities require a specific, scientific and systematic set of skills and techniques that leads to a successful performance of a player.

A sportsperson also needs special types of physical fitness components. These set of skills, techniques and components are achieved by training that further improves the performance of an individual. Hence, training is essential in the field of sports and physical education.

Meaning and Definition of Sports Training

The word 'training' means the process of preparation for some task. It is a process by which one gains practical and theoretical knowledge.

Training in sports means the preparation of a sportsperson based on the scientific principles for giving the highest level of performance. It is a specialised process of all-round physical strengthening aimed at improving an athlete's fitness in a selected activity.

Various definitions of sports training as given by scholars are as follows

- According to **Thiess and Schnabel**, "Sports training is a scientifically based and pedagogically organised process which, through planned and systematic effort, affects performance ability and performance readiness, aims at sports perfection and performance improvement as well as the contest in sports competitions."

- According to **Martin**, "Sports training is a planned and controlled process of achieving goals in which the changes of motor performance and behaviour are made through measures of content, methods and organisation."

- According to **D Harre**, "Sports training, based on scientific knowledge, is a pedagogical process of sports perfection which, through systematic effect on psycho-physical performance ability and performance readiness, aims at leading the sportsman to high and highest performance. Through active and conscious interaction with the given demands in sports training, the sportman's personality develops according to the norms and standards of socialist society."

Training is a long-term, systematic and a continuous process that recognises an individual's needs and capabilities to develop exercises based on scientific knowledge that enhances sports performance.

It develops basic and advanced skills, techniques, tactics, strategies, etc. for all sports activities and competitions.

Often, the concept of training and preparation coincide but they are not identical. While preparation is a broader and a complex term including training, nutrition, competitions, etc. Training is one part of preparation that includes fitness, safety, individual care, exercise, etc.

Concept of Sports Training

Sports training is a concept whose practice is spread over many years. Training method for a particular sport consists of training periods which are split into sessions and schedules.

These sessions and schedules are progressive in nature and training continues till mastery over a skill is achieved.

All training programmes are divided into three parts as discussed below

1. **Preparatory Period** This is the basic training programme wherein stress is given on basic fitness and skill for competitions. It is further divided into number of phases as follows

   - **Phase I** It includes various conditioning programmes that develops general abilities such as endurance, speed, strength, etc. taking about 6-12 weeks of practice. Training techniques include weightlifting, circuit training, running, etc.

   - **Phase II** In this phase, training focuses on mastery of advanced skills which continues for 4-8 weeks. Various techniques of specific games are also introduced in this phase.

   - **Phase III** In this phase, a player develops the tactics and strategies to be used under difficult situations like that of a competition. This phase continues over 2-5 weeks.

2. **Competition Period** In this period, the player achieves its top form and can participate in competitions to achieve top performance.

   Training, in this period, has maximum intensity. Sportspersons are trained technically and tactically with main focus on speed.

3. **Transitional Period** This period comes after the competition. In this period, a player relaxes and rests to recover from stress.

   The main purpose of this period is the maintenance of physical abilities for next competition.

Objectives of Sports Training

Training improves an individual's physical, psychological, intellectual and technical capacities and capabilities.

Training techniques have the following objectives

1. **Physical Preparation** Athletes need a holistic physical development as a training base as well as overall physical fitness. The purpose is to increase endurance and strength, develop speed, improve flexibility, and refine coordination, thus achieving a harmoniously developed body.

2. **Technical Preparation** Technical training involves developing the capacity to perform all technical actions correctly, perfecting the required technique, performing specific techniques and improving the technique of related sports while ensuring the ability to perform all movements correctly.

3. **Tactical Preparation** Tactical factors include improving strategy by studying the tactics of opponents, expanding the optimal tactics within athletes' capabilities, perfecting strategies, and developing a strategy considering future opponents.

4. **Psychological Preparation** Psychological preparation is also necessary to ensure enhanced physical performance. Psychological trainingimproves discipline, perseverance, willpower, confidence, and courage.

Principles of Sports Training

Sports training is based on certain scientific principles which guides the coaches, trainers and sportspersons to develop and implement suitable training programmes. These principles are generally agreed upon guidelines that are grounded in sport science and hold true in practice and competition.

The key sports training principles are as follows

1. **Priniciple of Continuity** Training should be a continuous process, as any break in training will reduce physiological capacity of the sportsperson. Training should be carried out on a regular basis without any long period of inactivity. However, there should be intervals of rest and recovery between training sessions.

2. **Principle of Balanced Training** This principle suggests that the right mix of training activities, diet and healthy lifestyle habits are required for optimal functioning.

   Going to extremes can result in poor performance, illness and injury. Overtraining, consuming too much of certain foods and nutrients (including water), or adopting crash diets are examples of imbalance.

3. **Principle of Individual Differences** It concerns adjustments in training based on differences between individual athletes. As different persons respond differently to exercise and load, their training programmes should be modified to take care of their differences.

4. **Principle of Overload** It provides guidance about intensity of workloads and increasing the workload after the body has adapted to the previous load.

   It means that the training loads should be increased for improving the performance of sportspersons. Once the load is adapted, it is no longer efficient. Hence, the load must be increased after a passage of time for continuous improvement.

5. **Principle of Rest and Recovery** It concerns rest and recovery between exercises and time gap between workouts. The body regenerates between training sessions and so intervals between them should be planned accordingly.

6. **Principle of Reversibility** It provides guidance about detraining when athletes stop working out. It says that sportspersons lose the beneficial effects of training when they stop working out.

   The physiological effects of fitness training diminishes over time, causing the body to revert to its pre-training condition. Conversely, it also means that detraining effects can be reversed when athletes resume training.

7. **Principle of Specificity** It tells how workouts change sportspersons' bodies to prepare for the demands of their sports. To become better in a particular skill, the sportsperson must train in that particular exercise or skill required in it. For example, Gymnasts require more flexibility training.

8. **Principle of Transfer** It provides guidance on how workout activities can speed up the athlete's results in competitive performances. It says that learning and performing one activity affects the performance of related skills and activities.

   This principle is essential for designing practice strategies that have the greatest positive impact on competitive performance. Correctly applying this principle saves valuable training time besides accelerating results.

9. **Principle of Variation** It provides direction about variations in exercises, rest time, intensity and other variables.

   As training occurs over a long period of time, it tends to become boring for both the sportsperson and the coach.

   Varying the training programmes helps to maintain the interest and motivation of the sportsperson.

   Further, introduction of new activities and including fun games into the session can prevent problems such as plateaus in performance and overtraining effects.

10. **Principle of Progression** According to this principle, the overload should not be increased too slowly or too rapidly as it may result in injury or muscle damage. Exercising above the target zone can be dangerous.

    The principle of progression also makes us realise the need for proper rest and recovery. The constant overload can lead to exhaustion and injury.

11. **Principle of General and Specific Preparation** For the improvement of performance, both the general and specific preparations are significant. General preparation serves as the base for specific preparation.

    The general preparation increases the functional capacity of all the body systems and organs while, specific preparation is required to improve those systems and organs, on which the performance of sportspersons directly depends.

12. **Principle of Active Involvement** The principle of active involvement means that for an effective training programme, the athlete must participate actively and willingly.

Various experts list describe sports training principles in different ways but the underlying concepts in all of them are essentially the same.

All of these principles work together in coordination with each other during sports training to effectively improve the performance.

Concept of Doping

The word 'doping' refers to the use of drugs in the field of sports to enhance the physical capacity of sportspersons. In general, it is the use of performance enhancing substances by the athletes or sportspersons to gain an advantage over competitors.

The concept of doping is not new in sports. In ancient Greece, there were specialists who would offer nutritional ingredients such as mushrooms, opium and other herbal beverages that enhanced sports performance. Even Gladiators are known to use various substances that aimed at enhancing strength.

In the modern times, the use of doping first came out in 1904 Olympics, when **Thomas Hicks** won the marathon race. He had taken injections of strychnine.

The increase in doping increased so much that in 1928, the International Athletic Association Federation banned doping followed by other sport federations.

With the introduction of synthetic hormones, the problem of doping worsened. As a result, sports federations all-around the globe, banned doping and emphasised on blood testing.

The International Olympic Committee started considering the "presence in the human body of substances which are prohibited according to the list published by the IOC and/or the international organisation" as illegal.

Soon, the **World Anti-Doping Agency** (WADA) was formed in 1999 which defined doping as "the occurrence of one or more of the anti-doping rule violations set forth in Article 2.1 through Article 2.8 of the code."

They set some anti-doping rules that identified doping as

- The presence of prohibited substances and methods.
- Use or attempted use of a prohibited substance or prohibited method by an athlete.
- Refusing or failing to submit sample collection after notification by the authority.
- Possession of prohibited substances or prohibited methods.
- Tampering or attempting to tamper with any part of the doping control process.
- Trafficking or attempted trafficking in any prohibited substance or prohibited methods.
- Failure to inform an athlete's whereabouts after being notified.
- Administering, or attempting to administer a prohibited substance or method to an athlete.

Therefore, doping refers to the substances that are prohibited by the authority.

Classification of Doping

Doping can be classified into the following two types

I. Performance Enhancing Substances

1. **Stimulants** These are the drugs that enhance alertness and physical activity by increasing heart rate, breathing rate and the functions of the brain.

   These include **adrafinil**, **ephedrine**, **cocaine** and various **amphetamines**.

   They stimulate both physically and mentally by reducing the feeling of fatigue and enhancing aggressiveness. They are taken through injection, nasal spray and orally.

2. **Narcotics** They are used to relieve pain and discomfort which could arise from muscle strain or an injury. They also reduce anxiety and help in making persistent efforts for a longer time.

   Narcotics such as **methadone, morphine, heroin,** pethidine, etc. are usually used during competition.

3. **Beta-2-Agonists** These drugs relax the muscles of the airway to allow more oxygen to come in during respiration. Athletes usually take these drugs to enhance respiratory function, increase the capacity for strenous activities and to shorten recovery time.

   All Beta-2-Agonists such as formoterol, salbutamol, etc. are prohibited, although they are easily available in the form of inhalers for asthma patients.

4. **Anabolic Steroids** They stimulate the growth of muscles and help athletes to train harder and recover quickly. Nandrolone, Drostanolone, Primbolan (also known as methenolone) and oxandrolone are some common anabolic steroids. These are taken orally or by intramuscular injection.

5. **Diuretics** They reduce weight rapidly by removing body fluids such as water. Though they cannot enhance performance, their use is illegal because they are used as masking agents for removing other doping substances. Dextran is an example of a diuretics.

6. **Peptide Hormones** These hormones are produced naturally by glands in the body. They increase muscle bulk, strength, and oxygen-carrying red blood cells.

   These include erythropoietin (EPO), human Growth Hormone (hGH), Insulin-like Growth Factors (IGF-1) etc.

7. **Glucocorticosteroids** These drugs are used for relief from fatigue and pain. They help in preparing athletes to continue their efforts for longer periods.

8. **Aromatase Inhibitors** They help in increasing testosterone secretion, thus giving more strength. Examples of such inhibitors are **Testolactone, Anastrozole, Formestane,** etc.

9. **Cannabinoids** They cause a feeling of relaxation. Athletes use them for speedy recovery after any exertion. Hashish and **Marijuana** are common Cannabinoids which are banned.

II. Physical Methods

It includes gene doping and blood doping

1. **Gene Doping** It is the manipulation of cells or genes for enhancing the body's sports performance. It is based on the principles of gene therapy.

   It plays a vital role in the growth of musculoskeletal structures. It helps in speedy recovery from tendon, ligament and muscle injuries.

2. **Blood Doping** World Anti-Doping Agency (WADA) defines blood doping as the misuse of certain techniques or substance to increase one's red blood cell count, which allows the body to transport more oxygen to muscles and therefore increase stamina and performance.

The method used in it includes taking out some blood from an athlete a few weeks before competition, freeze and store it till one or two days before the competition and then inject the blood back into the athlete.

This practice boosts red blood cells, raising the capacity of the blood to carry oxygen, thus enhancing the performance of the athlete.

This is called autologous blood doping. The injection of fresh blood in the body of an athlete from another person is called homologous blood doping.

Another way of blood doping is to inject artifical oxygen carriers including certain chemicals and proteins into the blood.

Prohibited Substances and Methods

Prohibited substances and methods are those that are not allowed to be used in competitive sports. WADA maintains and updates this list of prohibited substances and methods every year.

Some substances are banned only during competition whereas others are banned at all times. Some others may be banned due to the method of administration.

If any of these are required as a medicine, they must fulfil the conditions given below

- The athlete's health will be adversely affected if he does not take it.
- There is no suitable alternative to it.
- There is no considerable performance enhancing benefit by consuming this drug.

Substances Prohibited at all Times

According to WADA, the following substances are banned in all sports competitions

1. **Anabolic Steroids** Anabolic steroids such as drostanolone, metenolone, oxandrolone, tetrahydrogestrinone, stanzolol, etc. are prohibited as they enhance the performance of an athlete artificially and have serious side effects.

2. **Peptide Hormones** Peptide hormones such as erythropoietin, human growth hormone, insulin, human chorionic gonadotropin and adrenocorticotropic hormone, etc are banned as they artificially increase the muscle and produces excess red blood cells.

3. **Beta-2-Agonists** These are the substances that are generally prescribed for asthma patients. These are prohibited in all sports.

4. **Diuretics** All diuretics and masking agents are banned in and out of all competitions for giving athletes an unfair competitive edge, as these drugs are used in sports to remove fluids from the body and reduce weight rapidly.

5. **Hormones and Metabolic Modulators** Any substances that interfere with the function of hormones such as tamoxifen and comipherne are banned from all sports.

Methods Prohibited at all Times

WADA has prohibited three methods of doping athletes. These are as follows

1. **Manipulation of Blood and Blood Components** This category includes
   - Administration or reintroduction of any quantity of autologous, homologous or heterologous blood, or red blood cell products of any origin into the circulatory system.
   - Artificially enhancing the uptake, transport or delivery of oxygen through haemoglobin-based blood substitutes products, but not including supplemental oxygen by inhalation.
   - Any form of intravascular manipulation of the blood or blood components by physical or chemical means.

2. **Chemical and Physical Manipulation** This category includes
   - Tampering, or attempting to tamper the samples collected during doping control, including urine substitution or adulteration.
   - Intravenous infusions and/or injections of more than 50 ml per 6 hour period except for those legitimately received in the course of hospital admissions, surgical procedures or clinical investigations.

3. **Gene Doping** This category includes
   - The transfer of polymers of nucleic acids or nucleic acid analogues.
   - The use of normal or genetically modified cells.

Substance Prohibited in Competitions

Many substances are banned or prohibited only at the time of competitions. They are as follows

1. **Stimulants** Stimulants such as caffeine, amphetamines, ephedra, cocaine, etc. act on the central nervous system and improves the performance artificially. Hence, they are banned in competitions.

2. **Narcotics** Narcotics such as fentanyl, morphine and oxycodone are not allowed during competitions.

3. **Cannabinoids** Substances such as hashish, marijuana, etc. induces relaxation artificially and hence, are banned during all competitions.

4. **Glucocorticosteroids** Some pain relievers such as Betamethasone, Budesonide, Cortisone, etc. are banned from all competitions.

Apart from these, certain Beta-blockers such as Bisoprolol, Carteolol, etc are banned from
certain sports including Archery, Golf, Shooting, Skiing/Snowboarding and Underwater sports.

Side Effects of Prohibited Substances

The use of prohibited substances results in numerous problems. It may even be fatal for health. The side effects of such substances are as follows

1. **Anabolic Steroids** Overdose of steroids can have serious side effects including the risk of cardiovascular diseases, liver diseases and many behavioural changes. It affects the endrocrine systems and brings many physical changes.

   In males, female body developments like enlarging of breast becomes eminent. In females, facial hair, abnormal menstrual cycle is commonly observed.

   The intake of steroid results in extreme mood swings, aggression, depression etc.

2. **Beta-2 Agonists** The side effects are excessive sweating, headache, nauseal, muscle cramps, restlessness, rapid heartbeat etc. They also have some other side effects like reduction in potassium concentration in blood serum and increase in glucose level in the body.

3. **Hormone and Metabolic Modulators** They interfere with the body's endocrine system and enhance the risk of serious diseases. They also slow down some enzyme reactions causing hot flushes, excessive sweating, and loss of sleep.

4. **Stimulants** They are very harmful for the cardiovascular system. Blood pressure and body temperature increases due to narrowing of blood vessels and results in cardiac arrest. They can also cause respiratory paralysis and psychological problems.

5. **Diuretics** They disrupt the balance of water and salt in the body. This can lead to muscle cramps, acute hypertension and circulatory shock. Other side effects are gastrointestinal and kidney problems.

6. **Narcotics** They cause problems in coordination and concentration. Overdose of narcotics may lead to fatal respiratory paralysis.
   It can also cause a false sense of security and invincibility which is very fatal, as it leads to overtraining.

7. **Cannabinoids** They lead to a drop in physical performance and affect short-term memory. High doses cause anxiety, panic, restlessness and confusion. They reduce concentration and coordination, and can also cause heart diseases and lung cancer.

8. **Glucocorticoids** They affect the immune system which leads to decrease in bone density (osteoporosis) and muscle wasting, which increases the risk of injury.

9. **Alcohol** The consumption of alcohol leads to impairment of the thinking process. It can cause respiratory paralysis leading to death. Alcohol addiction damages cells of the body, besides affecting the nervous system and liver.

10. **Peptide Hormones** Their excess use can be fatal. The overdose of these hormones leads to heart palpitations, agitation, hypertension, diabetes etc.
    High intake of EPO causes thickening of blood which increases the risk of heart attacks, strokes and pulmonary embolism. Due to imbalance of these hormones, there could be osteoporosis, ulcers and cataracts.
    Further, it can lead to abnormal enhancement of body organs as well as low blood sugar levels which can cause brain damage and even death.

Chapter Practice

Objective Questions

• Multiple Choice Questions

1. Which period of training comes after competition?
   (a) Preparatory   (b) Competition
   (c) Transitional   (d) Technical

Ans. (c) Transitional period of training comes after competition. In this period, player gets recovery time and maintains physical ability for the next competition.

2. What is the full form of 'WADA'?
   (a) White Anti-doping Agency
   (b) Wide Anti-doping Academy
   (c) World Anti-doping Agency
   (d) None of the above

Ans. (c) The full form of WADA is World Anti-doping Agency. It was formed in 1999. It defined doping as "the occurrence of one or more of the anti-doping rule violations set forth in Article 2.1 through Article 2.8.

3. Women who take ...., tend to develop muscular bodies.
   (a) Beta-blockers   (b) Amphetamines
   (c) Diuretics   (d) Steroids

Ans. (d) Women who take steroids, tend to develop miscular bodies. Steroids are drugs that stimulate the growth of muscles.

4. Which of the following is the performance enhancing substance or method?
   (a) Blood doping   (b) Gene doping
   (c) Narcotics   (d) Autologos doping

Ans. (c) Narcotics is the performance enhancing substance. Blood doping, gene doping and autologos doping are physical methods of enhancing performance.

5. Alcohol stimulates the
   (a) Muscular system   (b) Digestive system
   (c) Nervous system   (d) Excretory system

Ans. (c) Alcohol stimulates the nervous system. Due to its consumption, brain and nerves become weak, neuromuscular coordination decreases and reaction time of such individuals increases.

6. Match the following

List I	List II
A. Adrafinil	1. Peptide hormone
B. Erythropoietin	2. Narcotics
C. Dextran	3. Stimulant
D. Pethidine	4. Diuretics

Codes

	A	B	C	D
(a)	3	1	4	2
(b)	4	2	3	1
(c)	2	3	1	4
(d)	1	4	2	3

Ans. (a) The correct match is A-3, B-1, C-4, D-2.

7. Match the following.

List I	List II
A. Anabolic Steroids	1. Nervous system
B. Cannabinoids	2. Endocrinal changes
C. Alcohol	3. Heart diseases
D. Beta-2 Agonists	4. Diabetes

Codes

	A	B	C	D
(a)	4	1	3	2
(b)	4	2	1	3
(c)	2	3	1	4
(d)	1	4	2	3

Ans. (c) The correct match is A-2, B-3, C-1, D-4.

8. The use of doping first came out in ______.
   (a) 1906   (b) 1904   (c) 1912   (d) 1940

Ans. (b) The use of doping first came out in 1904.

9. Joy, a boxer initially started taking certain drugs in small amount to increase his muscle power. But after some time, his body got a habit of it and now he takes it daily.

What should a doctor at medical camp suggest Jay?
   (a) Rapidly reduce stimulants intake.
   (b) Slowly reduce stimulants intake.
   (c) It is impossible to leave this habits.
   (d) Given away sports.

Ans. (b) Doctor at medical camp suggest jay to slowly reduce stimulants intake. Regular intake of stimulants makes it a habit. The habit should be reduced slowly by decreasing its intake.

10. Stimulants such as caffeine, amphetamines, ephedra, cocaine etc. act on the central nervous system and improves the performance artificially. This affects athletes health adversely.

How stimulants impact the performance of a sportsperson?
   (a) It reduces stress.
   (b) It removes tiredness.
   (c) It increases blood pressure.
   (d) All of the above

Ans. (c) The stimulants have a direct effect on the cardio vascular systems as they increase the heart rate thereby increasing the blood pressure.

11. You have noticed your friend using sports enhancing drugs for winning sports competitions. He says that he needs it for stimulation as winning the competition is very important for him. To explain him the side effects of taking drugs, select the best option from the following.
   (a) They are good pain killers.
   (b) They increase muscle mass.
   (c) They cause hyper tension.
   (d) They reduce anxiety.

Ans. (c) Stimulants raise the blood pressure and cause hyper tension which is an ill effect. Other options increase in muscle mass, reducing anxiety are positive.

• Assertion and Reasoning

Directions (Q. Nos. 1-4) *Each of these questions contains two statements, Assertion (A) and Reason (R). Each of these questions also has four alternative choices, any one of which is the correct answer. You have to select one of the codes (a), (b), (c) and (d) given below.*

Codes
   (a) Both A and R are true and R is the correct explanation of A
   (b) Both A and R are true, but R is not the correct explanation of A
   (c) A is true, but R is false
   (d) A is false, but R is true

1. **Assertion** (A) Sports training is planned and controlled process.

   Reason (R) Training is essential in the field of sports and physical education.

Ans. (b) The Assertion is true as sports training means proper planning, preparation of the process and a controlled way of practising.

Reason is also true as training is the first and the most essential step in the field of sports and physical education. It enhances sports performances. Thus, Both A and R are true, but R is not the correct explanation of A

2. **Assertion** (A) Stimulants are considered as drug.

   Reason (R) Gene doping is physical method of doping.

Ans. (b) The Assertion is true as stimulants enhance alertness and physical activity so they are considered as drug.

Reason is also true as Gene droping is when cells or genes are manipulated for enhancing sports performance. But reason do not explains assertion. Thus, Both A and R are true, but R is not the correct explanation of A.

3. **Assertion** (A) Cannabinoids are banned from sports competitions although they give relief from fatigue and pain.

   Reason (R) This practice boosts red blood cells raising the capacity of blood to carry oxygen therefore cannabinoids are banned.

Ans. (c) Assertion is true as Cannabinoids like Hashish and Marijuana are banned from sports competition. They cause a feeling of relaxation and pain relief. The reason is false as red blood cells are boosted by the physical method of blood doping while cannabinoids are performance enhancing substances. Thus, A is true but R is false.

4. **Assertion** (A) Principal of reversibility tells how adjustments based on individuals should be done.

   Reason (R) The overload should not be increased too slowly or too rapidly as it may result in injury or muscle damage.

Ans. (d) The assertion is false as principle of reversibility provides guidance about detraining when athletes stop working out.

The reason is true as overloading of training exercises should not increased too slowly or too rapidly to avoid any related injuries. Thus, A is false but R is true.

• Case Based MCQs

1. Prakash is the coach for the school Basketball team. During training sessions, he noticed that some players could continue exercises without fatigue for longer periods than others while some players have faster reaction time. He then split the students and gave different exercise and training schedules. Based on this case, answer the following question

(i) Which principle of sports training is observed by Prakash?
(a) Principle of balanced training
(b) Principle of Specificity
(c) Principle of Individual differences
(d) Principle of progression

Ans. (c) Prakash observed the principle of individual differences which states that response to exercise and training is different in everyone due to individual differences.

(ii) Which principle of training means that training sessions should consist of many variables?
(a) Principle of active involvement
(b) Principle of variation
(c) Principle of reversibility
(d) Principle of overload

Ans. (b) Principle of variation or variance means that training must be planned with different challenges and variables.

(iii) The principle of recovery means which of the following?
(a) Rest is important
(b) Training is continues process
(c) Intensity of workloads
(d) None of the above

Ans. (a) Principle of recovery means rest is important as rest is always required for the body to recover from exertion of training.

PART 2
Subjective Questions

• Short Answer (SA) Type Questions

1. Define sports training? Enlist the principles of sports training.

Ans. Training in sports means the preparation of a sportsperson based on the scientific principles for giving the highest level of performance. It is a specialised process of all-round physical strengthening aimed at improving an athlete's fitness in a selected activity.

The principles of sports training are
- Balanced training
- Individual differences
- Reversibility
- Specificity
- Progression
- General and specific preparation
- Active involvement

2. What are two reasons for the requirement of an effective training programme in sports? What is the result if they are not conducted?

Ans. Two reasons for the requirement of an effective training programme in sports are as follows
(i) Producing skillful high performers for success in major international competitions.
(ii) Development of healthy participants.
If such training programmes are not conducted, a sportsperson's potential will never be fulfilled. They will not be able to develop the skill and competitive edge needed to win a sports event. The sport persons will be weak in physical, technical, tactical and psychological preparation needed in winning a sports competition.

3. Explain any three principles of sports training.

Ans. Three principles of sports training are as follows
(i) **Principle of Balanced Training** It concerns achieving the right proportions between training activities and rest. It also relates to the body's tendency to return to normalcy or **homeostasis**.
(ii) **Principle of Individual Differences** It concerns adjustments in training based on differences between individual sportspersons.
(iii) **Principle of Overload** It provides guidance about intensity of workloads and increasing the workload after the body has adapted to the previous load.

4. Explain the three phases of preparatory period in sports training.

Ans. Preparatory period is the basic training program where stress is given on developing fitness and skill needed for sports competitions. The three phases of preparatory period are as follows
- **Phase I** This phase consist of programs that develop speed, strength, endurance. This phase includes 6-12 weeks of practice. Training of weight lifting, running and circuit training comes in it.

- **Phase II** This phase focus on mastery of advanced skills. It includes 4-8 weeks of practice and various techniques of specific games are introduced in this phase.
- **Phase III** This phase develops the tactics and strategies to be used under tough situations and consist of 2-5 weeks of practice.

5. What is Principle of Variation? How it enhances sports training?

Ans. The Principle of Variation provides direction about variations in exercises, rest time, intensity and other variables. It means to include a number of different activities and exercises in the training program to maintain the interest and motivation of the athlete. This can be done by changing the nature of exercise, increasing the time of each session, changing the group and environment, etc.

As training occurs over a long period of time, it tends to become boring for both the sportsperson and the coach.

Varying the training programmes helps in maintaining the interest of the sportsperson. Further, introduction of new activities and including fun games into the session can prevent problems such as plateaus in performance and overtraining effects.

6. "Doping has been a part of the field of sports since time immemorial". Justify the statement.

Ans. Doping refers to the use of drugs to enhance physical performance. The concept of doping is not new in sports.

In ancient Greece, there were specialists who would offer nutritional ingredients such as mushrooms, opium and other herbal beverages that enhanced sports performance.

Even Gladiators are known to use various substances that aimed at enhancing strength.

In the modern times, the use of doping first came out in 1904 Olympics, when Thomas Hicks won the marathon race. He had taken injections of strychnine.

After that, the increase in doping increased so much that in 1928, the International Athletic Association Federation banned doping followed by other doping federations.

Soon, the International Olympic Committee started considering the "presence of substances in the human body which are prohibited according to the list published by the IOC and/or the international organisation" as illegal.

Hence, it can be said that doping has been a part of the field of sports since time immemorial.

7. Elaborate the anti-doping rules of sport.

Ans. Anti-doping rules of sport are as follows

- The presence of prohibited substances and methods.
- Use or attempted use of a prohibited substance or prohibited method by an athlete.
- Refusing or failing to submit sample collection after notification by the authority.

- Possession of prohibited substances or prohibited methods.
- Tampering or attempting to tamper with any part of the doping control process.
- Trafficking or attempted trafficking in any prohibited substance or prohibited methods.
- Failure to inform an athlete's whereabouts after being notified.
- Administering, or attempting to administer a prohibited substance or method to an athlete.

8. Discuss the effects of stimulants both beneficial and harmful.

Ans. Stimulants are a class of drugs that stimulate the body's central nervous system which include the brain and spinal cord. They have, both beneficial and harmful effects like enhancing alertness and physical activity by increasing heart rate, breathing rate and the functions of the brain.

They stimulate both physically and mentally by reducing the feeling of fatigue and enhancing aggressiveness.

The harmful effects of stimulants increase in hypertension, anxiety and even respiratory paralysis and cardiac arrest.

Stimulants also has many toxic effects like they increase aggression and violent behaviours, cause dizziness, blurred vision and irregular heartbeat. They also cause addiction and increase dependance which can lead to intake of high doses of stimulants.

9. What do you mean by a prohibited substance? State the effects of using Betablockers and Peptide Hormones.

Ans. Substances which are not allowed to be used in sports by any sportsperson are known as prohibited substances. The use of these substances is illegal. Therefore, World Anti-doping Agency (WADA) has issued a list of prohibited substances.

The effect of using Betablockers is to relax the muscles of the airway to allow more oxygen to come in during respiration, which increases endurance. They also reduce blood pressure and heart rate in heart patients.

The effects of using Peptide Hormones are increase in muscle bulk, strength and oxygen-carrying red blood cells. However, they interfere with the working of estrogens (i.e. female hormones).

10. What constitutes manipulation of blood and blood components, according to WADA?

Ans. According to WADA, manipulation of blood and blood components includes

- Administration or reintroduction of any quantity of autologous, homologous or heterologous blood, or red blood cell products of any origin, into the circulatory system.

- Artificially enhancing the uptake, transport or delivery of oxygen through haemoglobin-based blood substitute products, but not including supplemental oxygen by inhalation.
- Any form of intravascular manipulation of the blood or blood components by physical or chemical means.

11. Explain the side effects of Cannabinoids, Glucocorticoids and alcohol.

Ans. (i) **Cannabinoids** They lead to a drop in physical performance and affect short-term memory. High doses cause anxiety, panic, restlessness and confusion. They also reduce the concentration and coordination power and can cause heart and lung diseases.

(ii) **Glucocorticoids** They affect the immune system which leads to decrease in bone density (osteoporosis) hence increasing the risk of injury.

(iii) **Alcohol** The consumption of alcohol leads to impairment of the thinking process. It can cause respiratory paralysis leading to death. Alcohol addiction damages the cells of the body, affecting the nervous system and liver.

12. List the substances that are banned in sports competitions but otherwise can be taken?

Ans. Many substances are banned or prohibited only at the time of competitions. They are as follows

(i) **Stimulants** Stimulants such as caffeine, amphetamines, ephedra, cocaine, etc. act on the central nervous system and improves the performance artificially. Hence, they are banned in competitions.

(ii) **Narcotics** Narcotics such as morphine and oxycodone are not allowed during competitions.

(iii) **Cannabinoids** These substances such as hashish, mariyuana, etc. induces relaxation artificially and hence are banned during all competitions.

(iv) **Glucocorticosteroids** Some pain relievers such as betamethasone, budesonide, cortisons, etc. are banned from all competitions.

13. Write a short note on blood doping.

Ans. World Anti-Doping Agency (WADA) defines blood doping as the misuse of certain techniques or substance to increase one's red blood cell count, which allows the body to transport more oxygen to muscles and therefore increase stamina and performance.

The method used in it includes taking out some blood from an athlete a few weeks before competition, freeze and store it till one or two days before the competition and then inject the blood back into the athlete.

This practice boosts red blood cells, raising the capacity of the blood to carry oxygen, thus enhancing the performance of the athlete.

14. Differentiate between autologous and homologus blood doping.

Ans. The difference between autologous and humologus are as follows

Autologous Blood	Homologous Blood
Autologous blood doping is when blood from an athlete is taken out, frozen and stored a few weeks before the competition.	Homologous blood doping is when fresh blood of another person is injected into the body of an athlete.
It is again injected one or two days before the competition. This boosts the red blood cells in the body and enhances performance.	This also increases red blood cells in the body and enhances performance.
In autologus own blood is used.	In homologous blood of some other person is used.

• Long Answer (LA) Type Questions

1. Explain in brief the meaning and concept of sports training.

Ans. Training in sports means the preparation of a sportsperson based on the scientific principles for giving the highest level of performance.

It is a specialised process of all round physical strengthening aimed at improving an athlete's fitness in a selected activity.

Training is a long term, systematic and a continuous process that recognises an individual's needs and capabilities to develop exercises based on scientific knowledge that enhances sports performances.

It develops basic and advanced skills, techniques, tactics, strategies, etc. for all sports activities and competitions.

Sports training is a concept whose practice is spread over many years. Training method for a particular sport consists of training periods which are split into sessions and schedules.

These sessions and schedules are progressive in nature and training continues till mastery over a skill is achieved.

All training programs are divided into three parts. These are as follows

(i) **Preparatory Period** This is the basic training program wherein stress is given on basic fitness and skill for competitions.

(ii) **Competition Period** In this period, the player achieves its top form and can participate in competitions to achieve top performance.

(iii) **Transitional Period** This period comes after the competition. In this period, a player relaxes and rests to recover from stress.

2. List five major categories of performance enhancing substances used by sports persons and explain their effects in one sentence each.

Ans. The categories of performance enhancing substances used by sportspersons are as follows

  (i) **Stimulants** They enhance alertness and physical activity by increasing heart rate, breathing rate and the functions of the brain, besides reducing the feeling of fatigue and enhancing aggressiveness.

  (ii) **Narcotics** They are used to relieve pain and discomfort which could arise from muscle strain or an injury, reduce anxiety and help in making persistent efforts for a longer time.

  (iii) **Beta-2-Agonists** These drugs relax the muscles of the airway to allow more oxygen to come in during respiration, which increases endurance.

  (iv) **Anabolic Steroids** They stimulate the growth of muscles and help athletes to train harder and recover quickly.

  (v) **Diuretics** They reduce weight rapidly by removing body fluids such as water and are also used as masking agents for removing other doping substances.

3. Describe briefly about the substances prohibited by WADA. Also explaining the reason for prohibiting them.

Ans. WADA has classified the prohibited substances into following categories

  (i) **Anabolic Steroids** Anabolic steroids such as drostanolone, matenolone, oxandrolone, etc. are prohibited as they enhance the performance of an athlete artificially and have serious side effects.

  (ii) **Peptide Hormones** Peptide hormones such as erythropoietin, human growth hormone, insulin, etc. are banned as they artificially increase the muscle and produces excess red blood cells.

  (iii) **Beta-2-Agonists** Substance that are generally prescribed for asthma patients, are prohibited in all sports.

  (iv) **Diuretics** All diuretics and masking agents are banned in and out of all competitions for giving athletes an unfair competitive edge.

  (v) **Hormones and Metabolic Modulators** Any substances that interfere with the function of hormones such as tamoxifen and clomiphene are banned from all sports.

4. What are the side effects of any five prohibited substances?

Ans. Five prohibited substances with their side effects are as follows

  (i) **Anabolic Steroids** Overdose of steroids can have serious side effects inducing the risk of cardiovascular disease, liver diseases and many behavioural changes.

It affects the endocrine systems and brings many physical changes. In males, developments such as enlargement of breasts happen, while in females, facial hair is commonly seen.

  (ii) **Beta-2-Agonists** Their side effects are excessive sweating, restlessness, rapid heartbeat, etc. They also have some other side effects like reduction in potassium concentration in the blood serum and increase in glucose level in the body.

  (iii) **Hormone and Metabolic Modulators** They interfere with the body's endocrine system and enhance the risk of serious diseases. They also slow down some enzyme reactions causing of flushes, excessive sweating and loss of sleep.

  (iv) **Narcotics** They cause problems in coordination and concentration. Overdoes of narcotics may lead to fatal respiratory paralysis. It can also cause a false sense of security and invincibility which is very fatal.

  (v) **Diuretics** They disrupt the balance of water and salt in the body. This can lead to muscle cramps, acute hypertension and circulatory shock. Other side effects are gastrointestinal and kidney problems.

• Case-Based Questions

1. Karan is an athlete. He completed the 400 m relay race, which he won. But after the decleration of the result, he was disqualified for doping charges. Based on this case, answer the following questions.

  (i) What do you understand by doping?

Ans. Doping means the use of drugs in the field of sports to enhance the physical capacity of the Athletes. It improves sports performance.

  (ii) What are the two methods of doping?

Ans. The two methods of doping are taking performance enhancing substances and altering the body by injecting or manipulating cells or genes.

2. In the preparatory period, there are three phases in which the players achieve their physical fitness and skill efficiency needed for the competitions. They are preparatory, competition and transitional period. The preparatory period also has three stages.

(i) Which period of training is a relaxing period?

Ans. The third phase i.e. transitional period of training is a relaxing period. It is also called off reason as player gets recovery from competition stress.

(ii) Which phase is the longest period of training?

Ans. The preparatory phase is the longest period of training. It has three phases and the total duration is 4-5 months. It prepares a player for an upcoming sports event.

3. Sanju wants to loose weight rapidly to take part in a boxing event. At the same time, he wants to improve his muscle mass. He has started taking diuretics and anabolic steroids. Based on this case, answer the following questions.

(i) What are diuretics?

Ans. Diuretics are used to remove fluids from the body to reduce body weight rapidly. They are used by boxers, wrestlers, weightlifters, etc.

(ii) What are the side effects of Beta-2 Agonists?

Ans. The side effects of Beta-2-Agonists are restlessness, rapid heartbeat, excessive sweating, reduction of potassium in blood serum and increase in glucose level etc.

Chapter Test

Multiple Choice Questions

1. Find the incorrect statement
(a) Sports training is a scientifically based program
(b) Sports training is a planned process
(c) Sports training is short term, static program
(d) Sports training is a systematic process.

2. _____ drugs relax the muscle of the airway to allow more oxygen to come in during respiration.
(a) Anabolic Steroids
(b) Beta-2-Agonists
(c) Narcotics
(d) Diuretics

3. .... is the physical method of doping.
(a) Gene doping
(b) Blood doping
(c) Both (a) and (b)
(d) Neither (a) nor (b)

4. .... provides guidance about detraining when the athletes stop working out.
(a) Principle of Reversability
(b) Principle of overload
(c) Principle of rest and recovery
(d) Principle of Transfer

5. Which among the following is a performance enhancing drug?
(a) Diuretics
(b) Cannabinoids
(c) Peptide Hormones
(d) All of the above

6. Rohit is a student of class XIth and is going through a stimulant's intake. During a recent medical check-ups at school he was advised to do certain things.

Based on this case, answer the following questions.

(i) Which part or system of body is highly prone to stimulants?
(a) Respiratory system
(b) Digestive system
(c) Cardiovascular system
(d) None of the above

Short Answer (SA) Type Questions

7. Explain the nature of sports training and differentiate it with preparation.

8. How is the principle of specific preparation different from general preparation?

9. The concept of doping is not new. Explain this statement.

10. What is the effect of steroids in sports?

11. Give the ill effects of narcotics.

Long Answer (LA) Type Questions

12. Explain any five principles of sports training in detail.

13. All training programs are divided into how many parts? Explain them.

Answers

1. (c) *2.* (b) *3.* (c) *4.* (a) *5.* (c) *6.* (c)

CBSE Term II
Physical
Education XI

Practice Papers
1-3

Practice Paper 1*
(Solved)

Case Based Questions

1. Rohit is a yoga instructor in a primary school. He noticed that young children are lacking in balance and coordination of their limbs. Therefore in his yoga class, he taught the children a particular asana that will help them to strengthen their limbs, back and also improve balance. The picture below shows the asana taught by Rohit to young children. (1× = 5)

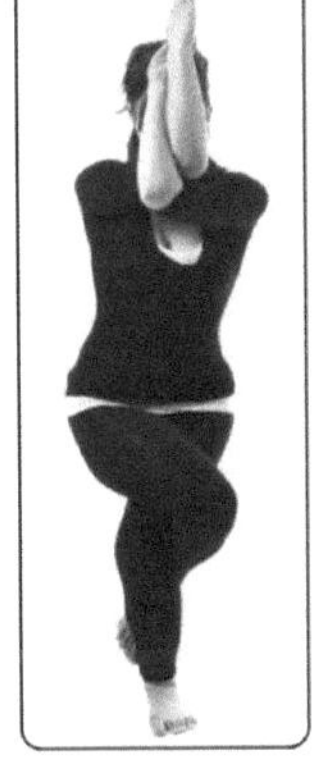

   (i) Name the asana shown in the image.
   (a) Tadasana (b) Shashankasana (c) Naukasana (d) Garudasana

   (ii) Which among the following is done is standing posture?
   (a) Vrikshasana (b) Naukasana (c) Sukhasana (d) Padmasana

   (iii) Eagle pose is the other name of which asana?
   (a) Sheershasana (b) Garudasana (c) Vajrasana (d) Halasana

(iv) Which among the following asanas help to improve coordination and balance?

(a) Garudasana   (b) Vrikshasana   (c) Both (a) and (b)   (d) None of these

(v) The asana, children can do to increase their height is _____ .

(a) Naukasana   (b) Tadasana   (c) Matsyasana   (d) Makarasana

Short Answer Questions

$(3 \times 5 = 15)$

2. Write a brief note on any three stages of the development.   (3)

Or 'Adequate independence' is crucial in management of adolescent problems. Examine.

3. Discuss Dharana and Dhayana.   (3)

4. Briefly explain any two principles of the sports training.   (3)

Or Define technique in sports and what are basis of its selection by or the player's.

5. If any team or organisation has a good and capable leader then team or organisation always perform good. Such leader will play what roles.   (3)

6. How sports psychology helps in learning motor skills?   (3)

Or What precautions need to be taken by while trekking.

Long Answer Questions

$(5 \times 3 = 15)$

7. Describe the role of professionals for children with special needs.   (5)

Or In what ways dream of Inclusion of children with the special need can cherished?

8. A leader is muti-dimensional in nature. What qualities make him/her multi-dimensional.   (5)

Or If school management ask you to go on any adventure sports. Then what it would be and what safety measure's you need to take.

9. "Warming-up is considered as most important in the sports arena." Examine   (5)

Or Dinesh is member of school football team. In order to boost his performance he has started consuming prohibited substance. What may be side effect of prohibited substance on his body.

Answers

1. (i) (d) The asana shown in the image is Garudasana. It is a standing balancing asana.

(ii) (a) Among the following, Vrikshasana is done in standing posture. Naukasana is done in lying posture. Sukhasana and Padmasana are done in sitting posture.

(iii) (b) Eagle pose is the other name of Garudasana. In Sanskrit, Garuda means eagle.

(iv) (c) Both Garudasana and Vrikshasana help to improve coordination and balance. They are done in standing posture.

(v) (b) Tadasana is the asana that children can do to increase their height. It is also called maintain pose.

2. The three stages of development are as follows

Early Childhood This stage starts at the age of 2 years and goes upto 6 years. As the most important period of growth and development, in this period, the child is a pre-school going toddler.

Late Childhood This stage lies between 6 to 12 years of age and is also referred to as troublesome age. It is also known as the gang age and children in this age are more influenced by their peers than anyone else.

Adolescence Spanning between 13 to 19 years, adolescence is a stage, when the individual becomes integrated with the society of adults by undergoing marked intellectual and sexual transformations.

This is a stage of complex changes which brings us to the stage that will end the childhood and lead to adulthood.

Or

Adolescents value freedom and independence. They want to express their views and feelings independently.

They desire to take their own decision and are irritated when any order or restriction is imposed on them. Hence, parents must give them adequate freedom and try to understand their sentiments.

Therefore, it can be observed that adolescence is the age of struggle. It is very necessary to give proper attention to them, so that they are able to manage their problems during this crucial phase of growth and development.

3. Dharana and Dhyana are elements of yoga. They are discussed below

Dharana

It is the concentration of the mind and the first stage of meditation. You focus all your energy at one point without letting your mind get distracted, and discard all your random thoughts. The mind is fixed on one subject, topic or place.

Dhyana

It is a process of complete constancy of mind. *Dharana* sets the stage for *dhyana*. When one starts focussing on a topic, the mind starts actively engaging with its focus.

Thus, *dhyana* is the active modification of knowledge in complete stability and calmness.

4. Two important principles of sports training are as follows

Principle of Individual Differences It concerns adjustments in training based on differences between individual athletes. As different persons respond differently to exercise and load, their training programmes should be modified to take care of their differences.

Principle of Overload It provides guidance about intensity of workloads and increasing the workload after the body has adapted to the previous load.

Or

A technique is the basic movement of a sport or event. It involves scientific and economical methods that tell a sportsperson how an action is performed so as to achieve top performance.

In other words, a technique in a sport is a sequence of movements that makes the performance better.

As there are a number of techniques that a player can use, a particular technique is selected by a player to suit his/her level. Any technique is selected by a player on the following basis

- Improves his/her performance
- Suites the skill level of player
- Be within the rules
- Be the best in the given circumstances

5. A good and capable leader will play following role to ensure success of any team or organisation.

- The role of a leader is to integrate the individual goals with that phf the organisation or team.
- The leader, with his intelligence, maturity and pleasing personality, helps the team members by providing them support and increasing cooperation.

- The role of a leader is to take strategic decisions for the success of the team as well as develop plans to realise those decisions.
- An important role is to make an impressive team that consists of people with different talents so that the team members assist each other instead of competing with each other.
- A good leader in sports is also a good organiser.
- A good leader makes sure that the plans are executed well.
- A good leader acts as an example for his/her team.

6. Sports psychology plays a major role in learning motor skills. Such a learning depends on the individual's level of readiness, *i.e.* both physiological and psychological readiness.

Physiological readiness in children is the development of the necessary strength, flexibility and endurance, while psychological readiness is related to the learner's state of mind, *i.e.* the desire and willingness to learn the particular skill.

Sports psychology plays an essential part in understanding psychological readiness and interests as well as attitudes of an individual towards efficient learning and performance of a motor skill.

Or

The following safety measures should be taken before and while taking part in this activity

- Avoid trekking during the rainy season or during bad weather. Before starting, check the weather report for the area where you are going and prepare yourself or your group (if any) accordingly.
- Take all the required materials like water, matchbox, food items, rope, sleeping bag, tent etc.
- To avoid insect bites, wear full sleeve shirts and full pants.
- Wear proper footwear so that you do not slip while trekking in hilly areas.
- Do not eat leaves, flowers etc. found on the wayside, as they may be poisonous.
- Take along a multi-pocket carry bag which is large enough to carry all the essential items.
- It is suggested that you use trekking stick for better and efficient trekking.

7. The professionals who work with children with special needs have to focus on their overall development. They help and support such children in achieving their full potential, giving ability to communicate properly, etc.

The roles of these professionals are discussed below

Counsellor A counsellor is a trusted professional who provides a safe and supportive environment. The role of the counsellor is to discuss the concerns of the child with special needs and understand the feelings, emotions and sentiments of the child.

A counsellor also counsels the parents, guardians and teachers of the child with special needs. He provides guidance and helps the child to adapt to different situations because he understands the mental and physical needs of the child.

Occupational Therapist An occupational therapist is a professional who helps the children with special needs to develop fine and gross motor skills like eating, dressing, bathing, drinking etc.

An occupational therapist also helps them develop their sensory and cognitive abilities. This is done by teaching simple activities like grasping, reaching, picking, dressing, feeding etc.

Physiotherapist The role of the physiotherapist is to manage children with movement disorders. He teaches them how to balance their movements while walking, rolling, sitting and crawling. For this, various exercises are taught that also prevent the development of deformities.

Another role of the physiotherapist is to encourage a child's independence and mobility, thereby helping in building self-esteem.

Physical Education Teacher Physical education teacher generally determines the abilities of students with special needs and also the procedures that may need to be implemented to support their participation in sports and physical fitness.

Or

The dream of inclusion of children with special needs can be achieved through the implementation of following principles/strategies.

Differentiated Instruction The instructions should be designed in such a way that they are easily understood by all the students. Means of instruction can include visual, auditory, kinesthetic etc.

Academic Support It means flexible, self-pacing and supportive environment that caters to differential learning patterns.

Welcoming Environment It refers to love and respect for all the children including children with special needs coming from different backgrounds and abilities, thus providing them a wholesome environment.

Building an Inclusive Community Children with special needs will grow up as independent individuals if they are supported by a community that understands them. So, building a community where these children are an equal part of it, is very important.

Aligning Goals and Objectives It means aligning the goals and objectives of educating children with special needs to the same standards set for educating normal children.

Flexible Approach The approach towards inclusive education should be flexible. This should be reflected in the teaching methods and materials provided to the students with disabilities.

8. A leader is multi-dimensional in nature because he/she possess certain qualities. The main qualities are as follows

Self Awareness Leaders must possess a vision along with knowledge about their own strengths and weaknesses, knowledge about skills and complete information about the vision.

Determination and Dedication Leaders should have the confidence to meet the challenges with firm determination and dedication. He/She should be devoted to the profession and must be able to face even the worst situations.

Intelligence Wisdom is very important for a leader to develop intuition and insight for future events. A leader should be intelligent enough to find out all possible solutions for a complex set of problems.

Strong Interpersonal Skills A leader must be social. He/She should possess essential social qualities such as cooperation, affections, brotherhood, sympathy, empathy, respect etc. He/She must have the ability to interact and work harmoniously with all team members.

Decision-making A leader of physical education should be able to take decision spontaneously. He/She should be able to look at the problems logically and must take decisions at the right time.

Energy and Enthusiasm A leader should be energetic and enthusiastic. He/She should be able to motivate and excite the players to give their best to the game.

Good Health and High Motor Capacity A leader in physical education should have good health and high motor fitness. He/She must display all the components of physical fitness such as strength, speed, endurance, flexibility, etc.

Or

If school management offers me any adventure game then I will choose rock climbing.

Rock climbing is an activity in which participants climb up, down or across natural rock formations or artificial rock walls. The goal is to reach the summit of a formation or the end point of a pre-defined route without falling. To successfully complete a climb, one must return to the base of the route safely.

As one of the most **dangerous adventurous** sports, rock climbing requires strong mental control, agility, flexibility, endurance and various coordinative abilities such as coordination, balance, etc.

Safety Measures During Rock Climbing

The following safety measures should be taken before and while taking part in this activity are as follows

- Don't climb higher than you are supposed to.
- Put the harness on the body correctly, so that you do not get tangled in the rope if you fall.
- If you are new to rock climbing, belay (*i.e.* fix a running rope round a rock to secure it) with an experienced climber.
- Use the right equipment like shoes, ropes, slings etc.
- Practise falling away from the rock wall (so you do not hit any rocks on the way down). You will fall sometimes, especially if you want to get better.
- Take small breaks in between attempts. Give yourself a chance to recover before climbing again.
- Practise correct technique. Many new climbers try to hang with their fingers and elbow; this technique wastes energy and isn't effective.
- Your arms should be used for shifting weight, not trying to hold yourself up with a tight grip.
- Watch experienced climbers to help you improve your own technique and climbing safety.

9. Warming-up is considered important because of following reasons

Increases the Body Temperature A proper warming-up exercises increase the body and muscle temperature. As the muscles are warmed-up, the speed with which the muscles functions is increased which ultimately improves the performance of an athlete.

Improves the Functioning of Muscular and Nervous System Warming-up increases the rate at which muscles relax and contract. It increases the speed of the nerve impulses and decreases resistance in muscle capillaries. Further, the neuromuscular coordination improves which increases the efficiency of sportspersons.

Increased Metabolism and Circulation Warming-up increases the speed of transfer of oxygen and fuel of tissues. It increases the metabolic rate which leads to higher energy levels. An increase in 0.5°C increases the metabolic rate by 7%.

Improves Sports Skills Warm-up increases flexibility, strength, speed and endurance of a sportsperson.

Reduces the Chance of Injuries Warming-up ensures that the muscles are well prepared for any competition. Further, an efficient nervous system improves and sharpens the reaction time. This reduces the risk of wear and tear as well as any injury.

Improves Performance Warming-up increases the concentration power of athletes which, alongwith efficient skills, makes one perfect the skills, techniques and tactics that helps in attaining success in sports.

Or

The use of prohibited substances results in numerous problems. It may even be fatal for health. The side effects of such substances on Dinesh body are as follows.

- **Anabolic Steroids** Overdose of steroids can have serious side effects including the risk of cardiovascular diseases, liver diseases and many behavioural changes. It affects the endrocrine systems and brings many physical changes.
- **Beta-2 Agonists** The side effects are excessive sweating, headache, nauseal, muscle cramps, restlessness, rapid heartbeat etc. They also have some other side effects like reduction in potassium concentration in blood serum and increase in glucose level in the body.
- **Hormone and Metabolic Modulators** They interfere with the body's endocrine system and enhance the risk of serious diseases. They also slow down some enzyme reactions causing hot flushes, excessive sweating, and loss of sleep.
- **Stimulants** They are very harmful for the cardiovascular system. Blood pressure and body temperature increases due to narrowing of blood vessels and results in cardiac arrest. They can also cause respiratory paralysis and psychological problems.
- **Diuretics** They disrupt the balance of water and salt in the body. This can lead to muscle cramps, acute hypertension and circulatory shock. Other side effects are gastrointestinal and kidney problems.
- **Narcotics** They cause problems in coordination and concentration. Overdose of narcotics may lead to fatal respiratory paralysis.

Practice Paper 2[*]
(Unsolved)

General Instructions

■ Time : **2 Hours**
■ Max. Marks : **35**

1. There are 9 questions in the question paper. All questions are compulsory.
2. Question no. 1 is a Case Based Question, which has five MCQs. Each question carries one mark.
3. Question no. 2-6 are Short Answer Type Questions. Each question carries 3 marks.
4. Question no. 7-9 are Long Answer Type Questions. Each question carries 5 marks.
5. There is no overall choice. However, internal choice have been provided in some questions.
   Students have to attempt only one of the alternatives in such questions.

** As exact Blue-print and Pattern for CBSE Term II exams is not released yet, so the pattern of this
paper is designed by the author on the basis of trend of past CBSE Papers. Students are advised
not to consider the pattern of this paper as official. It is just for practice purpose.*

Case Based Questions

1. In order to win the state level athletics championship, Mahesh practiced hard for many days. On the other hand, Mohan planned for a short cut. As a result, Mohan, won the event but was caught on doping charges. He was found to be having genetically modified cells that provided him greater stamina. Based on this case, answer the following questions. $(1 \times 5 = 5)$

(i) Which kind of doping technique was used by Mohan?
  (a) Physical manipulation
  (b) Gene doping
  (c) Manipulation of blood
  (d) Intake of diuretics

(ii) Which international agency provides guidelines on doping?
  (a) WADA
  (b) WHO
  (c) ILO
  (d) UNICEF

(iii) Which among the following substance is banned for use in all sports competitions?
  (a) Anabolic steroids
  (b) Beta-2-Agonists
  (c) Metabolic modulators
  (d) All of these

(iv) Substances like caffeine and cocaine are termed as ______.
  (a) Narcotics
  (b) Cannabinoids
  (c) Stimulants
  (d) Steroids

(v) Why do you think Mohan has chosen the path of doping?
  (a) To get fast results
  (b) To reduce stress
  (c) To face new challenges
  (d) All of these

Short Answer Questions   (3 × 5 = 15)

2. Explain any three objectives of the physical education.   (3)

Or Describe how cousellor help a child with special needs?

3. Briefly explain the following   (3)
   (a) Competition Period   (b) Transitional

4. What are main salient feature of the development?   (3)

Or Describe the cognitive characteristics of infancy.

5. Name and discuss important skills of the sports person.   (3)

6. Why it is important to control doping?   (3)

Or Is there need to promote adventure sports. Examine.

Long Answer Questions   (5 × 3 = 15)

7. Define 'Adventure sports' and what are main benefits of the adventure games?   (5)

Or In sports players are highly prone to injuries. What precaution they should take while sports.

8. Differentiate between adolescence and adulthood. Also enlist the important characteristics of adulthood.   (5)

Or It has been noticed that issue of adolescent is rising rapidly. Describe the cause of such rise.

9. Discuss the procedure, benefits and contraindications of Naukasana.   (5)

Or Why it is important for the students to do meditation and yogic kriyas.

Answers

1.   *(i) (b)*   *(ii) (a)*   *(iii) (d)*   *(iv) (c)*   *(v) (a)*

Practice Paper 3*
(Unsolved)

General Instructions

- Time : **2 Hours**
- Max. Marks : **35**

1. There are 9 questions in the question paper. All questions are compulsory.
2. Question no. 1 is a Case Based Question, which has five MCQs. Each question carries one mark.
3. Question no. 2-6 are Short Answer Type Questions. Each question carries 3 marks.
4. Question no. 7-9 are Long Answer Type Questions. Each question carries 5 marks.
5. There is no overall choice. However, internal choice have been provided in some questions. Students have to attempt only one of the alternatives in such questions.

** As exact Blue-print and Pattern for CBSE Term II exams is not released yet, so the pattern of this paper is designed by the author on the basis of trend of past CBSE Papers. Students are advised not to consider the pattern of this paper as official. It is just for practice purpose.*

Code Based Questions

1. A group of 6 boys are going on a trekking. They all have packed their bags with food, water, rope, tents, sleeping bag and medicines. They have chosen a 10 kilometre trek along the high mountains. They have decided to go during the month of August to enjoy the natural beauty of the greenery in the mountains. Based on this case, answer the following questions. $(1 \times 5 = 5)$

(i) Trekking is a kind of ____.

   (a) Leisure sport   (b) Adventure sport

   (c) Competitive sport   (d) All of these

(ii) In the question, the kind of trek that is going to be undertaken is ________.

   (a) Easy trekking   (b) Difficult trekking

   (c) very easy trekking   (d) Moderate trekking

(iii) Which of the following material is not required in trekking?

   (a) Axe   (b) Raft

   (c) Stick   (d) Compass

(iv) Trekking should be usually avoided in which season?

   (a) Rainy   (b) Summer

   (c) Winter   (d) Autumn

(v) Which safety measure should be followed during trekking?

   (a) Fix a running rope around a rock to secure it   (b) Always wear a life vest and helmet

   (c) Work on your ground handling always   (d) Check the weather report before starting.

Short Answer Questions $(3 \times 5 = 15)$

2. Analyse the importance of sport psychology. (3)

Or Why it is important to given sex education to students?

3. Explain the type physiological warming-up in brief. (3)

4. How a person can a quire leadership qualities? (3)

Or What is the role of group leader in a trekking expedition?

5. Describe benefit of any two yogas of your choice. (3)

6. Explain any three types of surfing. (3)

Or In what way style is important in sports.

Long Answer Questions $(5 \times 3 = 15)$

7. If any one is going to start sports training then what principle they need to followed? (5)

Or Doping has become big challenge for regulating authority of sports and also discuss types of doping.

8. Define asana and describe different types asanas. (5)

Or Discuss adventure sport 'paragliding' and enlist the safety measures required for it.

9. Write short note on the following. (5)
   (a) Speech therapist   (b) Special Educator
   (c) Physiotherapist   (d) Counsellor

Or What are the different problems faced by adolescents? Explain in detail.

Answers

1.   *(i) (b)*   *(ii) (d)*   *(iii) (b)*   *(iv) (a)*   *(v) (d)*

Printed by Libri Plureos GmbH in Hamburg, Germany